MW01291665

The Trees Will Clap Their Hands

A GARDEN THEOLOGY

JON HUNTZINGER

WESTBOW
PRESS

WestBow Press books may be ordered through booksellers or by contacting:

WestBow Press
A Division of Thomas Nelson
1663 Liberty Drive
Bloomington, IN 47403
www.westbowpress.com
1-(866) 928-1240

All Scripture quotations are from The Holy Bible, English Standard Version® (ESV®), copyright © 2001 by Crossway, a publishing ministry of Good News Publishers. Used by permission. All rights reserved.

Any people depicted in stock imagery provided by Thinkstock are models, and such images are being used for illustrative purposes only.

Certain stock imagery © Thinkstock.

ISBN: 978-1-4497-3453-4 (sc)
ISBN: 978-1-4497-3455-8 (hc)
ISBN: 978-1-4497-3454-1 (e)

Library of Congress Control Number: 2011962789

Printed in the United States of America

WestBow Press rev. date 01/23/2012

To the memory of my grandfather, Oliver Huntzinger, who manifested the garden in everyday life.

And to my students, who ask good questions.

Contents

Preface

This study began a number of years ago with presentations I put together for a course on Old Testament Introduction at the King's University. At that time I also taught a course on the book of Genesis and another entitled Jesus and the Old Testament. In teaching these courses, I discovered that students were keenly interested in the Garden of Eden. But they did not cooperate with me and ask questions that I had so diligently prepared myself to answer. They wanted to know what kind of garden it was. Where was it located? What happened to it? And why do so many paintings of the garden depict an apple as the fruit that Eve ate? Such questions from inquiring students forced me to look more closely at the story of the garden and ask my own questions. After that time, it became common for me to make remarks about the garden in whatever classes I was teaching, from Hermeneutics to Jesus the Steward of the Kingdom to Pneumatology. The garden kept showing up. Some of those observations are given here.

I would like to thank my students for asking so many good questions over the years. I have learned much from them and it is to them that the book is dedicated. Thanks to Roy Hayden for his careful reading of the manuscript. Special appreciation goes to Steve Sisler for his creative design of the book. I am grateful for the time and talent they gave to the project. I am also grateful for the time that my wife, Penney, gave to the book in reading and editing the manuscript. She sees things that I don't see, and her suggestions substantially improved the book.

Abbreviations

OLD TESTAMENT

Gen.	Genesis
Exod.	Exodus
Lev.	Leviticus
Num.	Numbers
Deut.	Deuteronomy
Jos.	Joshua
Judg.	Judges
1 Sam.	1 Samuel
2 Sam.	2 Samuel
1 Kgs.	1 Kings
2 Kgs.	2 Kings
1 Chr.	1 Chronicles
2 Chr.	2 Chronicles
Neh.	Nehemiah
Ps./Pss.	Psalms
Prov.	Proverbs
Eccl.	Ecclesiastes
Song	Song of Songs
Isa.	Isaiah
Jer.	Jeremiah
Ezek.	Ezekiel
Dan.	Daniel
Hos.	Hosea
Jon.	Jonah
Mic.	Micah
Hab.	Habakkuk
Zeph.	Zephaniah
Hag.	Haggai
Zech.	Zechariah
Mal.	Malachi

NEW TESTAMENT

Matt.	Matthew
Rom.	Romans
1 Cor.	1 Corinthians
2 Cor.	2 Corinthians
Gal.	Galatians
Eph.	Ephesians
Phil.	Philippians
Col.	Colossians
Heb.	Hebrews
1 Pet.	1 Peter
2 Pet.	2 Peter
Rev.	Revelation

1

Introduction

From earliest times, people have planted gardens for food, beauty, retreat, and self-expression. We have exerted control over nature by giving shape to it through the making of gardens. That this was true in the past when most people lived in rural places and were close to the land only points to the significance of gardens today as more of us live in cities rather than in the country. In fact, ours is the first generation in human history in which more people live in urban areas rather than rural ones.[1]

More of us live closer together than ever before and farther from the land that produces the food we eat and displays the beauty that inspires us. In our cities, we are connected by mass communications and mass transit, enjoy a substantial standard of living due to mass production, and are influenced in beliefs and behaviors by mass marketing. Yet despite these marvels, we face new and massive challenges due to life together in large metropolitan areas. One way that we are responding to these challenges today is by planting more gardens than ever before.

When I think of gardens, I recall the very different ones that each of my grandfathers planted. Both men worked blue-collar jobs—the one as a self-employed auto-mechanic and the other a factory worker—and both found renewal in their gardens. My one grandfather planted a small tomato garden behind his house each summer. Weeding, watering, breaking up the hard ground—nothing gave him more pleasure than working a small backyard plot of ground not more than thirty feet by ten feet. My other grandfather worked thirty-five acres of meadows and woodland alongside Lake Manitouwabing in Ontario, Canada, that he had purchased after years of saving money from his job. He spent most weekends in a secluded place where he cleared the shore of driftwood, removed fallen trees and planted new ones, and built small cabins that would be his livelihood in retirement. Though neither possessed any special knowledge of soils or seeds or seasons—and neither would have called himself a gardener—both built gardens after a fashion. One was a backyard gardener in a working-class neighborhood where he grew tomatoes, and the other a north-woods gardener amidst a beautiful acreage of fields, trees, and rocky waterfront where he built cabins. Neither garden was cost-effective. The one produced just enough tomatoes to complement the meals my grandmother cooked, the other barely enough income on which to live in his later years.

So why did these two men plant their gardens? They planted them to escape the hard, noisy, mechanical worlds in which they worked and to find quiet, solitude, and rest in a different kind of work and world than the ones in which they lived week in and week out. Even so, their gardens represented something more to them than tranquility and refuge. They connected these men to the natural world, and through the natural world to the spiritual one, replenishing their souls in a way that they could not experience otherwise. The connection between land and human sustenance, self-understanding, and renewal is an old truth, to be sure. It is also a biblical one *Adam* as seen in the fact that the Hebrew word *'ādām* (Adam) is related to *'adāmāh* (ground or land). God created Adam from *'adāmāh*. The gardens my grandfathers planted grounded them in a deeper understanding of themselves as it has for men and women over the centuries.

It seems funny to suggest that my grandfathers had anything in common with someone like King Nebuchadnezzar of Babylon, whose hanging garden is still written about today. Or that there was any shared bond between them and Louis XIV, who oversaw the building of Versailles and its geometric gardens, or even the American renaissance patriarch Thomas Jefferson, who personally designed Monticello and its gardens. It seems laughable to consider that their gardens are in any way related to the most famous of all American gardens, Central Park in New York City, which was designed by Frederick Law Olmstead and Calvert Vaux as a refuge and place of rejuvenation for nineteenth century New Yorkers,[2] or can be compared to the Huntington Library garden close to my home in Southern California, which is a place of carefully cultivated beauty, diversity, and imagination. Yet as garden designer and historian Wade Graham observes, "Every good garden is a window— into the individual mind or minds of its makers, owners, inheritors, or inhabitants, and, through their stories layered on top of one another, a window to the collective mind, our common experience."[3]

More famous than any of these is the most ancient of all gardens described in the book of Genesis. The influence of the Garden of Eden and its story is hard to overestimate. It has provided and continues to provide a picture into our collective human experience. It isn't surprising, then, that allusions to humanity's first garden have been common throughout the history of western culture. Artists, writers, and composers have all drawn on the story of this garden and Adam and Eve for their creative works. The Arthurian legend of Camelot reprises the story of the garden, and John Steinbeck's novel *East of Eden* along with Cormac McCarthy's modern American classic *No Country for Old Men* both draw on it as well. The most famous of all literary works to draw on the garden and its story, undoubtedly, is John Milton's *Paradise Lost*.

The influence of the garden and its story is not limited to human art, literature, and music, however. This first story of the Bible becomes the thesis story that informs all that follows in the Scriptures. The biblical narrative of Israel—from the patriarchal period of Abraham to the period of the kings and prophets, and continuing into the ministry of Jesus and the mission of Paul—only makes sense in view of this first story. This study traces the imagery and meaning of the Garden of Eden throughout the Bible. It identifies a continuum of ideas related to the garden in subsequent passages of the Old and New Testaments and follows the chronology of the biblical story from creation to patriarchs to exodus to exile in the Old Testament and on to Jesus, Paul, and concluding with John's vision of the New Jerusalem in the book of Revelation in the New.

2

The First Garden

A Place of Provision

The story of the Bible begins with a description of creation and the planting of a garden. "And the Lord God planted a garden in Eden, in the east, and there he put the man whom he had formed" (Gen. 2:8). A careful reading of the whole passage indicates that the garden God plants should not be viewed merely as paradise or a place of pleasure, despite the fact that many of us think of it exactly in this way. This is the result of the Septuagint's translation, *paradeisos*, from the Persian *pairi-daeza* or "pleasure park."[4] Most depictions of the Garden of Eden advance this notion and show it to be tropical and lush, full of color, and teeming with wildlife.[5] And it is common for us to think of Eden as an idyllic, carefree place where the man and woman whiled away their time eating sweet fruit and frolicking with the animals. This vision is advanced by Milton when he lyricizes, "They sat them down, and, after no more toil//Of their sweet gardening labour than sufficed//To recommend cool Zephyr, and made ease//More easy, wholesome thirst and appetite//More grateful, to their supper fruits they fell,//Nectarine fruits, which the compliant boughs//Yielded them, sidelong as they sat recline//On the soft downy bank damasked with flowers."[6]

If the garden is not merely a place of pleasure or an Idyllwild, then what kind of place is it? Genesis paints an unexpected picture. It is a plantation of trees. "And out of the ground the Lord God made to spring up every tree that is pleasant to the sight and good for food. The tree of life was in the midst of the garden, and the tree of the knowledge of good and evil" (Gen. 2:9). This verse describes a grove or orchard of beauty, sustenance, life, and knowledge.[7] Beauty in that the trees of the garden are pleasant to view; sustenance in that the fruit of the trees is good to eat; life that is provided by one tree in the center; and knowledge that is represented in another. The garden is a place where humanity's most basic needs and desires are satisfied. It is where God provides for our need of beauty, physical nourishment, relationship with Him, and an understanding of how to live.[8]

The next verse expounds upon this picture of the garden by describing it as a well-watered land. "A river flowed out of Eden to water the garden, and there it divided and became four rivers." Flowing water represents health, growth, and life; it is fresh and pure and to be contrasted in our thinking with water that is stagnant and insipid.

Furthermore, it is abundant and provides enough water to fill four tributaries. The garden is a place of increase and the expansion of life. Surrounding the garden is a land where gold and other precious stones and metals are found. So, the description of the Garden of Eden is of a place of beauty, knowledge, and flourishing life that is encircled with wealth and treasure. The passage says nothing about indulgent pleasure or self-gratification. Instead, it speaks of abundant provision for aesthetic, physical, and intellectual needs of the man so that he may fulfill the grand purpose to be God's image (Gen. 1:26–27). It speaks of life in relationship with God and in connection with the world He has created.

A Place of Purpose

Into this wooded garden of beauty, provision, knowledge, and abundant life, God places *'ādām* to take care of it. "The Lord God took the man and put him in the Garden of Eden to work it and keep it" (Gen. 2:15). The Hebrew words for *work* and *keep* (*'ābad* and *šāmar*) suggest that there is something more to Adam's responsibilities than simply being a tenant farmer on God's property. He is responsible for sustaining and cultivating the rich resources of the garden. Presumably, this involves watering, fertilizing, pruning, and harvesting the fruit of the trees of the garden that provide for his four-fold needs. This means that Adam's responsibilities include developing the potential of the garden and its trees to inspire, nourish, enlighten, and give life.

Of course, this language is figurative, and it is significant that both *'ābad* and *šāmar* are frequently used in biblical passages that describe the sacrificial worship that priests performed at the tabernacle and temple. The word '*ābad* connotes the idea of service while the word *šāmar* indicates devotion.[9] They describe one who will minister and devote himself to God by fulfilling his responsibility within the garden. "The man is put in the Garden to worship God and obey him. The man's life in the Garden was to be characterized by worship and obedience; he was to be a priest, not merely a worker and keeper of the Garden."[10]

Not only this, but the garden is also a place where Adam is given responsibility to protect what God has planted. According to Peter Leithart, "Adam was formed and placed in Eden's garden with instructions to perform a priestly service that was also quasi-military. He was to 'dress and guard' the garden ... He was to keep intruders from the garden of God."[11] This insight adds to our grasp of Adam's responsibilities. Not only is he responsible for cultivating the richness of the garden like a gardener and for worshiping God through such devotion, but he is also responsible for preserving and protecting what God has created. There is manifold purpose to Adam's life.

Viktor Frankl, in his well-known and influential book, *Man's Search for Meaning*, draws upon his knowledge of human personality as a psychiatrist and his experience in Nazi concentration camps to observe that people desire meaning more than they desire pleasure or power. It is what he calls "the will to meaning." With respect to prisoners in the camps, he writes: "Woe to him who saw no more sense in his life, no aim, no purpose, and therefore no point in carrying on. He was soon lost."[12] Having a purpose in our lives is vital to living and flourishing at all times and in all places. Without it, we diminish and eventually die. Adam is created for a purpose: he is created to care for, preserve, and release the potential of God's creation, and he is created to praise and worship God. He has specific responsibilities in the garden, both toward God in worship on the one hand and toward His creation in preservation and cultivation on the other; it is in fulfilling these twin responsibilities that he would live.

Surprisingly, one way that Adam worships and praises God and fulfills his purpose is by naming the animals. "So out of the ground the Lord God formed every beast of the field and every bird of the heavens and brought them to the man [in the garden] to see what he would call them. And whatever the man called every living creature that was its name" (Gen. 2:18–19). This remarkable story should not be viewed as simple whimsy or serendipity, as though God amuses himself by discovering how clever His game warden proves himself to be. Adam's act of naming animals represents a way of knowing.[13] We name what we know and we gain knowledge through observation, inquiry, analysis, and reflection. Observation involves concentration and identifies the particular nature of something; inquiry asks questions; analysis discerns similarity and dissimilarity between one thing and another by making distinctions and establishing connections; reflection thinks about the meaning of the new knowledge gained; and description takes what is learned and makes it available to others by putting a name on it. And even as knowledge is built upon the past and what is already there, it also is directed to the future and what may yet exist, which is why C. S. Lewis says that knowing involves studying all the things that something can become.[14] Naming involves hard work in that it represents the culmination of learned knowledge even as it involves faith in its expectation of new things. Adam is not placed in the garden at the head of a line of animals, making up words for them as they parade before him. He is given responsibility for observing, learning about, and describing God's creations. In this way, he *Adam* worships God in the exploration and discovery of His creations through discipline, diligence, and faith.

Animal trainer Vicki Hearne draws from her years of working with dogs and horses to comment on the importance of giving and speaking names to them. She says that there must be a reason for giving names, otherwise we wouldn't do so. Despite advances in culture, nothing can replace the importance of giving names, and in training animals it is vital. She writes, "[No] advance will enable me to call Drummer Girl (a horse) with anything less than her name, which is why obedience training is centrally a sacred and poetic rather than a philosophical and scientific discipline."[15] Hearne says that naming animals is "sacred" and infers it to be a spiritual activity. She says that not to name or not to be able to name is to be something less than human—something less than Adam was created to be. Naming is a dutiful and privileged priestly exercise that distinguishes the role human beings have within God's creation from all others. It is a vital characteristic of being human.

Prior to the creation of living things, God names the light, darkness, expanse, dry land, and waters as *day, night, heaven, earth,* and *seas.*[16] This divine act of naming signifies the establishment of order over the formlessness and chaos that is described with the Hebrew words *tōhû* and *bōhû* in Genesis 1:2. It is important that God does not name the plants or animals in the story. The earth sprouts vegetation and the seas swarm with living creatures, but the plants and sea creatures and birds and land animals go unnamed.[17] The Hebrew word for *naming* in Genesis 1 (*qārā'*) is the same one used to describe Adam's responsibility to the animals in Genesis 2. "So out of the ground the Lord God formed every beast of the field and every bird of the heavens and brought them to the man to see what he would call (*qārā'*) them. And whatever the man called (*qārā'*) every living creature that was its name" (Gen. 2:19). Adam is to follow God's example. This means that he will extend order over the living world that God has made and act as a steward of it. All of this occurs in the garden, making it the place where Adam fulfills his priest-like responsibility to name, and grows in his understanding of the Creator.

By being placed in the garden and expected to engage in garden-keeping activities, Adam resembles the garden's designer. Wade Graham comments, "What makes gardens especially interesting … is that making one constitutes the creation of a new world—our own world, often nearly from scratch, an Eden where outside stresses, failures, and compromises can't enter."[18] Adam not only cultivates the garden that God has planted and protects it from outside destruction, but by naming the animals he participates in God's creative work and acts as a sub-creator.[19]

This purpose is grounded in the divine covenant that God makes with himself in the beginning. Though the Bible records several covenants between God and His people throughout the history of Israel—including what scholars describe as the Adamic, Noahic, Abrahamic, Mosaic, Davidic, and New Covenants—they all derive from a prior one. They represent permutations of the divine determination of God to be represented in creation through Adam. This means that all the covenants God makes throughout history with His people issue from a first divine covenant: "Let us make man in our image, after our likeness ... So God created man in his own image, in the image of God he created him; male and female he created them" (Gen. 1:26–27).[20] We were created to be God's image in the garden as a sub-creator who at the same time worships Him by learning about and taking care of His created world.

A Place of God's Presence

Provision and purpose are not the only blessings to be found in the Garden of Eden. To quote Graham again: "[A garden's] function is essentially social."[21] Thus, when the writer of Genesis says that God planted a garden, he depicts God as a gardener and it is presumed that He digs, plants, waters, prunes, uproots, and performs the many jobs that such a person does. [22] Yet, God does all of these things in order to create a space for a relationship. He wants a relationship with Adam and makes a place of provision and purpose wherein His presence can be known. It also means that Adam is a social being who thrives in a place of inspiration, nourishment, enlightenment, and life represented by the trees, where he can experience the presence of God and have a relationship with Him.

Presence is related to purpose. Viktor Frankl recalls how thoughts of his wife and his love for her sustained him during his harsh imprisonment. Her imagined presence kept him going and taught him "that love is the ultimate and the highest goal to which man can aspire … I understood how a man who has nothing left in this world still may know bliss, be it only for a brief moment, in the contemplation of his beloved. In a position of utter desolation, when man cannot express himself in positive action, when his only achievement may consist in enduring his sufferings in the right way … in such a position man can, through loving contemplation of the image he carries of his beloved, achieve fulfillment."[23] This is a beautiful expression of a profound truth. The presence of a loved one, or even the recollection of one's presence, can bring *bliss*, to use Frankl's word. Adam is placed in the garden to know the loving presence of God the gardener, who tends to him and cultivates purpose in his life.

This picture of God as a gardener is found throughout the Old Testament. For example, in Exodus, we are familiar with the Song of Moses and its famous description of God as a warrior who delivers Israel with His mighty right arm (Exod. 15), but we sometimes forget the additional description given by the psalmist: "You brought a vine out of Egypt; you drove out the nations and planted it. You cleared the ground for it; it took deep root and filled the land" (Ps. 80:8–9). This image of God as gardener is not romantic. It does not show God in an unrealistic way since ancient people knew too well, as do gardeners today, the hard work involved in planting and growing gardens. The image of God as a gardener conveys a picture of one who plans, works hard, gets dirty, and is patient in the cultivation of a place of life. It is an image that is implied by the remark that God moved about the garden (Gen.

3:8). Here at the end of the day, God walks in His garden to take pleasure in it like any gardener. He is present to enjoy it and the relationship it allows Him to have with Adam.

This relationship is qualified by Adam's respect for the word that God speaks to him. It is important to see the garden as a place of God's word or commandment. After planting the garden and setting Adam in its midst, God gives him responsibility and requires his obedience. The responsibility is to tend the garden; the requirement is to obey God's command: "You may surely eat of every tree of the garden, but of the tree of the knowledge of good and evil you shall not eat, for in the day that you eat of it you shall surely die" (Gen. 2:16–17). This word of knowledge complements the earlier command to increase and rule: "Be fruitful and multiply and fill the earth and subdue it and have dominion over the fish of the sea and over the birds of the heavens and over every living thing that moves on the earth" (Gen. 1:28). Adam is expected to live by God's words in that they represent an extension of God's own being and presence. The garden is a place where God speaks His word to Adam, and Adam enjoys God's presence as it is known through His word.

A Place of Proportionality

The opening chapter of Genesis describes the creation as good and implicitly but clearly reveals the God of creation to be good as well. Six times it reports God's response to His creation, "And God saw that it was good," and it concludes by declaring the work of God to be very good: "And God saw everything that he had made and behold, it was very good."[24] The lesson to be learned from the good creation is that the Creator himself is good. Adam will learn about His goodness by working in the garden and naming the animals. Discovery of the world is intended to lead to the discovery of that world's Creator.[25] It is hard work and requires discipline and faith; yet, it is the way of worship and it is the reason that God creates Adam.

God's work does not end there. When He compares Adam to the animals, He says, "It is not good that the man should be alone; I will make a helper fit for him" (Gen. 2:18). Eve is formed to help Adam exercise dominion over the created world and serve with him as a worshipper of God within that world. For the good work that God has accomplished to continue, Adam will need her help. The importance of Eve's ministry may be seen in the Hebrew word for helper. Rather than connote an idea of simple assistance, 'ezer points to necessary and vital service. It is a term that is used in numerous biblical passages to describe God's service to Israel so that Israel may be the priesthood to the nations. These passages define God as a helper to Israel who provides the protection, strength, and wisdom Israel needs to carry out her calling.[26] Without God's assistance, the people cannot fulfill their divinely given responsibility; and without Eve, Adam cannot reflect God's image or fulfill His ultimate purpose for the created world. God's goodness is manifested in the formation of Eve to be a helper to Adam. Only Adam and Eve, together, will display God's image and complete His purposes.

Thus, the idea of goodness connotes fulfillment of intention even as it involves the notion of proportionality. For God to declare creation to be good is for Him to say that everything is in proportion to His intention. It is very good in that Adam exists as man and woman and lives in a place exactly designed to sustain his life and to give him the opportunity to know God on the one hand and to cultivate the potential of the created world of which he is a part on the other. This is known in physics as the anthropic principle, which, according to astrophysicist Hugh Ross, is the scientific observation that "the universe has all the necessary and narrowly defined characteristics to make human life possible."[27] He writes, "The biblical depiction of Eden reveals a human habitat unexcelled in human comprehension, at least not within our current reality's limits. Eden represents the best environment possible for the human race within the space-time continuum of the cosmos."[28] As the trees of the garden reveal, this is true not only of Adam's physical life but also his social, spiritual, and intellectual life as well.

The connection between goodness and proportionality is also evident in what the ancient Greeks called the Golden Ratio. They observed order in the universe and sought to explain this order through ideas and numbers. One number that exhibited this perfect universal order was the ratio 1.618/1. They called this number the *logos*, which, according to Juliette Aristides, they saw as "the unifying principle of the universe." She explains: "Looking at nature, we see much variety. However, probe deeper into nature and we see a dominant proportional ratio responsible for much of its design … This ratio produces an order of such seemingly great intelligence that it was considered sacred by those who understood it."[29] This number explains what appears pleasing or proportional to human senses in everything from plants to galaxies to bird songs to the human body. The universe and all of the life within it gives evidence of its Creator.

Jesus identifies this principle of proportionality with human behavior in the kingdom of God, in what we now call the Golden Rule, when he tells his disciples, "Whatever you wish that others would do to you, do also to them, for this is the Law and the Prophets" (Matt. 7:12). This principle expresses the essence of the good life that his followers are to live. When we live in such a way, we not only experience the goodness of God's garden but we maintain it for others and offer worship to God in doing so. It is a life of balance and proportion.

The garden that God plants in Eden is a place of goodness and proportionality where His provision of beauty and abundance is enjoyed, where His purpose for Adam in discovery and worship is realized, and where His presence is experienced through His word. It is the place that becomes the model for future descriptions of the land promised to the people of Israel, and it is a paradigmatic place for all of us today by which we can judge our own places to see if they reflect God's original design.

Privation and Pain outside the Garden

Adam was created to know and experience God's goodness through obedience; he only experiences privation when he is expelled from the garden for disobedience.[30] He was to be inspired by beauty, strengthened with fruit, and animated with life from the trees of the garden, but he was to be enlightened through obedience to God's word and not by eating of the Tree of Knowledge. According to Lewis, obedience is the highest human virtue and disobedience the lowest human vice.[31] When someone or something obeys its natural superior and rules its natural inferior, there is proportion and goodness; when the opposite is true, there is disproportion and evil.[32] By rebelling against God's command and failing to obey his natural superior, Adam also fails to rule his natural inferior and allows disorder to manifest. Rather than leading the created world in praise of God and causing the trees to rejoice, from this time forward he struggles against the creation that he was intended to lead.[33]

But this is not the only sad result. The alternative to hierarchy is not equality but tyranny. Adam abrogates his responsibility to defend the garden and is demoted.[34] After he disobeys God's command, he is forced out of the garden: "[T]he Lord God sent him out from the garden of Eden to work the ground from which he was taken. He drove out the man." (Gen. 3:23–24). The significance of this is that Adam was created to know God and worship Him in the garden. He was responsible for manifesting God's image and extending the abundance of the garden throughout the rest of the created world by being fruitful. As Adam increased so also God's image would have increased in that world. The result of his disobedience, however, is that God's image is defaced, the ground is cursed, and "in pain you shall eat of it all the days of your life; thorns and thistles it shall bring forth for you" (Gen. 3:17–18). No longer will Adam eat fruit from the trees of the garden; now he will eat plants grown from the cursed ground. He has given up God's good provision for the product of his own labor, and he will live in a land of his own making.

Increased pain is descriptive of Adam's experience outside of the garden. First, God says to the woman, "I will surely multiply your pain in childbearing; in pain you shall bring forth children" (Gen. 3:16). God already has commanded Adam, "Be fruitful and multiply and fill the earth and subdue it and have dominion over the fish of the sea and over the birds of the heavens and over every living thing that moves on the earth" (Gen. 1:28). As he lives and increases, he is to nurture the life of the earth. He is to maintain proportion in the created world. This certainly would involve discipline, effort, and some pain. This command has not changed, but Adam's position has. He now must attempt to fulfill this command outside the garden, away from God's ample provision, clearly understood purpose, and direct presence. He will attempt to fulfill it through an abnormal experience of pain. Second, God says to the man, "Because you have listened to the voice of your wife and have eaten of the tree of which I commanded you, 'You shall not eat of it,' cursed is the ground because of you; in pain you shall eat of it all the days of your life" (Gen. 3:17). Man will not only experience pain in fulfilling God's command to increase, but he also will be forced to provide for himself from the ground in pain instead of enjoying God's good provision from the trees. The Hebrew word for *pain* (*'izzābôn*) is related to the verb for *shape* or *fashion* and to the noun for *idol*. Here it describes Adam's fruitless endeavor to provide or make for himself what God had already given to him.

To be cut off from the past is to be disinherited.[35] Adam cuts himself off from his past life in the garden when he eats from the Tree of Knowledge and, in doing so, is disinherited from the place of provision that God intended for him. He becomes a prodigal who is alienated from God and His presence. And whereas God's purpose was for him to know beauty, experience strength, increase in understanding, and live life, as well as to bear His image and likeness in the world, Adam's transgression interferes with all of this. God is not worshipped and His image is not refracted in the earth. Adam becomes confused and serves himself, leaving creation unfulfilled to groan and await the renewal of his inheritance as an adopted son of God.[36]

3

Abraham's Garden Journey

Men and women live in this condition for generations until the coming of Abraham.[37] The story of Abraham is a story about one Mesopotamian man who leaves his country, people, and family—all those social relationships that give him identity, motivate him with purpose, and support him with provision—for a distant land. In a sense, Abraham leaves the social space of his home for a faraway garden where he will know God's presence, discover new purpose, and enjoy bountiful provision. When God calls Abraham, who is Abram at the time, He promises to bless him and exalt his name in such a way that all people will be blessed through him (Gen. 12:1–3). This describes God's purpose for leading Abraham to a new land, and his obedience to this purpose results in divine provision. We read, "Now Abram was very rich in livestock, in silver, and in gold … And Lot, who went with Abram, also had flocks and herds and tents, so that the land could not support both of them dwelling together; for their possessions were so great that they could not dwell together" (Gen. 13:2–6). Abraham prospers because he is responding to God's prompting and is embracing His purpose to bless all nations. The ultimate provision made for Abraham, however, is that of God's own presence: "Fear not, Abram, I am your shield; your reward shall be very great" (Gen. 15:1). Abraham moves from place to place, but everywhere he goes, he builds altars to the Lord in worship. At each place he experiences God's prosperity and presence, anticipating the fulfillment of God's purpose in his life to bless the nations.

Another way that the narrative of Abraham recalls the story of the garden is in its treatment of Isaac. God's purpose for Abraham is seemingly in jeopardy when He demands that he offer the boy as a sacrifice. How can the nations be blessed if Abraham doesn't have a son through whom the blessing will come? Yet Abraham responds to the unthinkable by saying, "Here I am," and by hiking up Mount Moriah. When he arrives at the summit, God provides a substitute sacrifice so that Isaac may live and be the means through which Abraham is a blessing to all people. We read, "And Abraham lifted up his eyes and looked, and behold, behind him was a ram caught in a thicket by his horns." The importance of this provision is highlighted by the fact that Abraham declares a new name for God: "The Lord will provide" (Gen. 22:14). Here is the goal of serving God in the garden. It is not simply to name the animals of creation but to know and name God himself. Abraham knows God as "the Lord who will provide" in a way that he did not know Him in his home country among his own people.

In this way, the story of Abraham reveals the garden to be a place of proportion. Just as Abraham began his sojourn by exemplifying trust in God's word, so also he ends it in the same way. As a young man, he leaves country, town, and home for a promised land—a land that God will show him—only to come to the end of his travels as an old man to do the very same thing by climbing Mount Moriah to offer his son as a sacrifice. Whereas his identity and purpose as a young man was tied to his family and community, as an old man his identity and purpose is tied to his son and descendents. And in the same way that he was willing to leave his old identity for a new one when he was young, Abraham is willing to leave his new identity for yet a newer one still when he is old. The affirmative response to God's word when he was young in Mesopotamia is matched by his "Here I am" in the land of Canaan.[38] The world in which Abraham journeys is a land of proportion that is measured by the word that God speaks. Abraham believes in that word, and, in his acceptance of and engagement with it, he opens his life to God's blessing and shows his alignment with God's purposes.

4

The Exodus and the Garden

A Land of Milk and Honey

There are numerous ways in which the land of Canaan is viewed by the writers of Scripture: it is the wealthy land of a divine king, an inheritance for God's people, an actualization of divine covenant, a place to experience Sabbath rest, and a refuge for immigrants.[39] One important way that the land of Canaan is viewed is as a new Garden of Eden. When God promises to deliver the Hebrew people from slavery in Egypt, He says that He will lead them to "a land flowing with milk and honey."[40] Such a description of the land is more than a poetic picture of Israel's future home. It is a figurative way of recalling the original garden created by God for Adam that suggests He will abundantly provide for Israel just as He did for

Adam in Eden. Those who were once rich and then were poor will become rich again.

A land flowing with milk and honey vividly suggests a place of God's blessing and plentiful provision. For milk and honey to be produced, there must be sufficient water and grasses for the animals as well as water and moderate climate for fruit trees that are pollinated by bees for honey. The Hebrew word *debaš* does not necessarily mean bee-produced honey either, but may refer to any sweet substance and describe a type of sweet, thick syrup made from grapes, dates, or figs.[41] And it should be noted that the land is not said to be *rich* in milk and honey, nor is it described as *full of* milk and honey; rather, it *gushes* with milk and honey. The Hebrew term *zûb* is figurative and recalls the garden through which four rivers flow. It is also the same word used by the psalmist when he describes the time that God struck the rock, causing water to gush out of it for the people in the wilderness (Ps. 78:20). The promise God makes is that there is powerful provision for the people in the land. They will not be able to contain the abundance of His blessing.

So great is the miracle of the Exodus that it is compared to the day when Adam was created by God. As the Israelites camp on the plains of Moab and prepare to enter Canaan, Moses urges them to think back on the meaning of their forty-year wilderness journey: "For ask now of the days that are past, which were before you, since the day that God created man on the earth, and ask from one end of heaven to the other, whether such a great thing as this has ever happened or was ever heard of" (Deut. 4:32). The implication of the allusion to Adam is that God has been forming a new people for a new garden in the

Exodus. The years of wandering have been as the original days of creation, which concluded with the formation of Adam and his placement in the first garden. Given this fact, the people can look forward to Canaan being ample and rich like that one. It is a land "with great and good cities that you did not build, and houses full of all good things that you did not fill, and cisterns that you did not dig, and vineyards and olive trees that you did not plant" (Deut. 6:10–12). The people will inherit a land with everything they need to prosper, just as Adam was placed in a garden that provided everything he needed to live and worship God. If the people keep the commandments of God in the land, they will flourish: "He will love you, bless you, and multiply you. He will also bless the fruit of your womb and the fruit of your ground, your grain and your wine and your oil, the increase of your herds and the young of your flock, in the land that he swore to your fathers to give you … And the Lord will take away from you all sickness, and none of the evil diseases of Egypt, which you knew, will he inflict on you" (Deut. 7:12–15). These passages address a generation of people who are preparing to enter a new garden as a new people, very much like Adam, who was placed in the garden in the beginning. At this momentous moment, Moses reminds them of the miracle that they are living so that they will keep the commandments that God has given them and experience His provision as they fulfill His purpose.

God's purpose is not for the people to live indolent and satisfied lives, however. It is not so they can be perpetually merry, eating tart pomegranate pie and drinking sweet wine. So why does God promise abundant blessings for Israel? He does so for the same reason that He provided for Adam. He provides so that Israel may worship Him. Time after time, Moses asks pharaoh to release the people so they may go into the wilderness to worship, and time after time, Egypt's king refuses.[42] And when God promises to deliver the people and give them an abundant land, He says that the sign of His promise will be the worship they give to Him at Mt. Sinai (Exod. 3:12). The sign is fulfilled when the people gather at the base of the mountain to receive the covenant. There, God explains to Moses that He has brought them out of Egypt for the purpose of being a "kingdom of priests and a holy nation" (Exod. 19:6). He has brought them out in order to worship Him and lead the nations in worship as well.

Israel will worship God and experience His presence as they live out the commandments of His covenant. In fact, as theologian Samuel Terrien points out, "Presence is that which creates a people." He goes on to say, "The validity of the covenant depends upon the hearing of a voice … the obeying of a formulated word. The covenant has to be kept, observed, preserved, maintained. It is conditional. Initiated by presence, it leads to presence. Out of all peoples, the new people will become Yahewh's 'special treasure.'"[43] In this way, Israel will follow Adam, who worshiped God by keeping His commandment and by naming the animals. The ten words (*debarîm*) of the covenant are representative of God's presence and the means by which they will live in relation with Him and with one another in the land.[44]

Provision and Dietary Restriction

When God placed Adam in the garden, He provided all that he needed to carry out his priestly responsibilities.

30

God gave him a plantation of trees from which to eat and be strengthened for his work. Adam could eat from all of the trees but one. The fact that he could not eat from that one tree, however, represented a divinely imposed dietary restriction upon him. As long as he abided by this restriction, he would live in the garden and fulfill his duties.

one tree ↓

God places a similar restriction upon Moses and the Israelites. When He limits the amount of manna that they may gather in the wilderness, He places a requirement upon them. The people may collect enough manna to eat each day, but they may not collect and store it for future days. They are to trust in God's daily provision for their needs. As they learn to trust God for the continued provision of the manna, they will learn to trust Him with respect to the Torah and in this way be prepared for the restriction of what they can and cannot eat when they enter Canaan.[45] The people have to learn to live and abide by God's commandments while in the wilderness so that they may enter the Promised Land as a worshipful people obedient to His word. The time for learning God's commands is when they are outside the land; the time for living in compliance with those commands is when they are inside. This correlates with the story of Adam in the garden in that Adam lived in the garden as long as he obeyed God's commands. Once he disobeyed these, he was forced out. Moses and the Israelites will dwell in the land as long as they obey God's commands, including those that specify what foods they may and may not eat.

We have already seen that Adam was committed to the possibilities of God's creation by naming the animals, which was an expression of faith, and that he showed faith in God's word by not eating from the Tree of Knowledge. His life started out as one of obedience, worship, and faith. Likewise, the Israelites are to be a people of obedience, worship, and faith in the new garden in Canaan. Yet judgment will come upon them in the land if they fail to live by all of God's commands. It is not a coincidence that the purpose for their deliverance is made known to them at Sinai when they are given the commandments: "You shall be my treasured possession among all peoples, for all the earth is mine; and you shall be to me a kingdom of priests and a holy nation" (Exod. 19:5–6). Again, if they fail to obey all of God's commands, including those related to His provision for their needs, they will be removed from their garden—the land of milk and honey.[46]

What is the purpose of these restrictions? Why does God withhold the fruit of Tree of Knowledge? Why does He restrict how much manna may be gathered by the people? Why does He forbid the Israelites to eat certain meats? The answer has to do with the role that restraint plays in creation and sub-creation. Insight on this comes from artist Cor Blok, who comments on his paintings of scenes from J.R.R. Tolkien's *The Lord of the Rings*: "They are not projections of whatever images Tolkien's text conjured up before my mind's eye," he says. "They are pictographs, not photographs." These pictographs are unusual and sparingly descriptive. Interestingly, Blok did not decide beforehand upon a specific style and then go about depicting the stories in that manner, but rather, "it all went rather more spontaneously and haphazardly, once I had come under the spell of Tolkien's creation." In fact, his "pictorial vocabulary"—the style of the pictographs—was drawn from several different sources related to another project. What he learned from that project and Tolkien is "that 'style' is not necessarily something that grows naturally from an artist's personality or from some collective unconscious. A style is in fact a set of rules … which restricts your movements but challenges you to make the utmost of what is allowed, exploring possibilities where no one has seen them before. Consequently, one may consciously *adopt* a set of rules to serve as a 'style,' even temporarily for a specific purpose." Anyone familiar with Blok's work would agree that the result is a new and compelling way of seeing Middle Earth.[47]

What Blok discovered about his art is useful for understanding proportionality and interpreting the limitations placed on Adam in the story of the garden. The imposition of the limitation of style did not hinder Blok's retelling of Tolkien's story. Instead, it opened a new and remarkable way of experiencing that world. Blok's style resulted in new possibilities for thinking about Hobbits, elves, and orcs. Likewise, the limitations imposed upon Adam were not intended to keep him from fulfilling his responsibilities but provided him with the opportunity "to make the most of what is allowed [and to] explore possibilities where no one has seen them before." In a way that strikes us as counterintuitive, the limitations of the garden were designed to lift the limits and make possible God's desire for Adam to have dominion over the creation. By refusing to live with the limitations imposed upon him, however, Adam limited the possibilities that God created for him to experience. This was true for Israel in the land, and it is true for God's people at all times. By living in harmony with God's word—by living in proportion to the parameters that He establishes for our lives—the possibilities of life increase and multiply for us.

Garden Symbolism in the Tabernacle

In the book of Exodus, we read detailed instructions for the construction of the tabernacle by Moses and the Israelites.[48] The tabernacle stood in the center of the camp and represented God's presence in the midst of His people, in the manner of an ancient Near Eastern warrior-king who would pitch his tent in the center of his army. It was built with the most valuable materials possessed by the people. Precious stones, rare metals, select woods, and fine fabrics were gathered from the people, who used their skills to cut, saw, sew, design, form, fashion, and set the furnishings and equipment of the tabernacle. All of their treasure, talent, and time went into the construction of the tabernacle, making it a true representation of the people themselves. After all, what better represents people's lives than the things they treasure, such as heirlooms and the time that they devote to learn trades or hone talents to support themselves? By having the people contribute these things to building the tabernacle, God showed that He intended to personally inhabit their very lives.

The tabernacle was divided by a blue, purple, and scarlet curtain into two rooms, one at the front and one at the back. The room at the front contained a lamp stand, a table, and a golden altar, and the room at the back contained the Ark of the Covenant.[49] The front room symbolized a type of garden: the lamp stand signified God's presence with the people, the table signified God's provision, and the altar signified the purpose of worship. More precisely, the lamp stand was fashioned in the shape of an almond tree to represent the Tree of Life and God's continued presence in the midst of their wandering.[50] Also, even as God had provided for Adam in the garden, so also the table of presence was a symbol of His continuing provision for them. (The offerings that were placed on the table were possible because of God's provision.) And even as He had given responsibility to Adam to work and keep the garden as a priest, so also the golden altar reminded the Israelites that they were to be worshippers. Wherever the tabernacle went, there went the garden.

The garden was also represented in the Ark of the Covenant that was located in the back room, known as the Most Holy Place. This sacred chest held the Ten Commandments, Aaron's budded almond rod, and manna.[51] Like the furnishings of the tabernacle, these objects recalled the spiritual dimensions of purpose, presence, and provision experienced by Adam in the garden: the Ten Commandments represented the way the people were to live as a kingdom of priests, even as Adam was invested with priestly authority in the garden and expected to live by God's command; Aaron's budded rod symbolized the life-giving nature of God's presence with the people and recalled the Tree of Life in the garden; and the manna represented God's provision for the people in the wilderness just as He had made abundant provision for Adam. The ark represented, in miniature, the garden where God was present with His people (budded rod) to provide (manna) all they needed to fulfill His purposes (commandments).

Temple Worship and the Garden

Solomon's temple was built in the tenth century B.C. several hundred years after Israel settled in Canaan and then rebuilt after the Babylonian exile. Like the tabernacle, this temple also represented the garden of God. It was the place where the purpose of leading the nations in the worship of God ultimately would occur. Both psalmists and prophets envisioned the nations making their way to Jerusalem to give their offerings at the temple where the priests of Israel would preside. To this end, the construction of the building, along with its furnishings and symbolic art, recalled the garden. For example, ten lamp stands gave the impression of a grove of trees even as pictures of palm trees and flowers decorated the wood-paneled walls of the holy place. "Everything [in the temple] reminded people that this was a special place, a new creation of God in a world that was corrupt and contaminated. This was his other Eden, the place where heaven and earth met, the earthly replica of the heavenly sanctuary of God."[52]

Also, the temple was viewed as a place of God's presence where the people experienced renewal of relationship with Him and with one another through the ritual of sacrifice (provision) in their worship (purpose). Many of the psalms that were sung at the temple as part of this worship exult in God's word that provides blessing, calls for praise, and speaks of His presence. Psalm 19:7–11 is one of these that succinctly states the garden principle of blessing that follows obedience to God's word: "The law of the Lord is perfect, reviving the soul;//The testimony of the Lord is sure, making wise the simple;// The precepts of the Lord are right, rejoicing the heart;//The commandment of the

Lord is pure, enlightening the eyes;//The fear of the Lord is clean, enduring forever;//The rules of the Lord are true, and righteous altogether.//More to be desired are they than gold, even much fine gold; //Sweeter also than honey and drippings of the honeycomb.//Moreover, by them is your servant warned;//In keeping them there is great reward."

Here the psalmist uses a variety of terms to describe the value of God's word and the "great reward" that is given in keeping it. It well describes Adam's garden experience in that he was given the commandment of God and enjoyed the great reward of abundant provision by obeying it. All the people who sang these words at the temple would have been conscious of the privilege they had been given to enjoy God's great reward by remaining faithful to the laws, testimonies, precepts, commandments, and rules of His covenant. Personal revival, wisdom, and enlightenment were free gifts as they listened to and lived by God's word and experienced His presence through it.

Other songs reminded the people that they could relive Adam's experience of God's presence in their own lives as they kept the words that God had given to them in the Torah. For example, Psalm 1 declares that the person who delights in the law of the Lord will be "like a tree planted by streams of water that yields its fruit in its season, and its leaf does not wither. In all that he does, he prospers." The psalmist says that by making God's word a priority in their life and welcoming the presence of God through His word, the people will receive provision so that they can be productive. Another psalm proclaims that righteous people—people who faithfully live by the commands of the covenant—will "flourish like the palm tree and grow like a cedar in Lebanon. They are planted in the house of the Lord; they flourish in the courts of our God. They still bear fruit in old age; they are ever full of sap and green" (Ps. 92:12–14).

The people will flourish in the presence of God as they attend to His word and fulfill the purpose for which they were called by giving a testimony to the nations. In a well-known psalm of David, God is envisioned as leading a procession to the temple where He will receive the praise of both His people and the nations. The psalmist exults, "Because of your temple at Jerusalem kings shall bear gifts to you ... Nobles shall come from Egypt; Cush shall hasten to stretch out her hands to God. O Kingdoms of the earth sing to God; sing praises to the Lord, to him who rides in the heavens, the ancient heavens" (Ps. 68:28–35). All of this occurs because the nations see divine blessing in the power and strength that God has bestowed upon His people as they remember His mighty acts and live by His word.

Not only did the people of Israel experience the garden in faithful response to the commandments of God's covenant, but they anticipated a future garden-like life in the house of God. The Twenty-third Psalm, in particular, expressed this hope. Memorably, it declares that the Lord is David's shepherd who leads him to green pastures and quiet waters. At the same time, it says the Lord is a royal host who seats David at a table overflowing with wine. Not only does He provide all that David needs and desires, but He also is present with David at all times, even during times of duress and darkness. The Lord's presence and provision is not given to him, however, so he can recline at the table and laugh at his enemies. Rather, the Lord anoints David's head with oil so that he might continue to rule his people. As the people and priests sang this song, they identified with David and imagined the garden of God's provision, purpose, and presence in terms of a verdant pasture and a royal banquet hall.

Even as the symbolism of the temple called to mind the garden of God, with the lamp stands and engravings of trees reminding the people of that pristine place of God's presence with Adam, the ritual of sacrifice and the singing of songs reaffirmed their purpose to be men and women of worship. Many of the songs drew attention to the importance of keeping the Torah and living by God's word so that they might continue to enjoy His blessing and provision and remember their calling to the nations.

5

The Trees Will Clap Their Hands: The Garden in Isaiah and Ezekiel

The Trees Clap Their Hands

The memory of the garden remained in the imagination of the prophets of Israel during the years of upheaval and exile that began with the Assyrian assimilation and continued through the Babylonian deportation. It firmly shaped the messages they proclaimed to the people as they looked with hope to the future. One of the best-known of these messages was delivered by Isaiah to God's people far away from the land of their ancestors, in exile, with no way of return (Isa. 55).

Seemingly, the message is too good to be true. It declares that there is water for those who are thirsty and food for those without money. Wine and milk are amply available. The people are urged to eat what is good and delight themselves with rich food. Not only does the prophet promise provision but he also reminds them of their purpose when he recalls God's covenant with David: "I made him a witness to the peoples, a leader and commander for the peoples. Behold ... nations that did not know you shall run to you, because of the Lord your God, and of the Holy One of Israel, for he has glorified you." The nations will hurry after Israel when God leads them back to their own land.

The prophet recognizes that this is too much for an uprooted and dislocated people to absorb: "My thoughts are not your thoughts, neither are your ways my ways, declares the Lord. As the heavens are higher than the earth so are my ways higher than your ways and my thoughts than your thoughts." What is clear is that this promise of provision and purpose is certain since God has spoken it: "For as the rain and snow come down from heaven and do not return there but water the earth, making it bring forth and sprout, giving seed to the sower and bread to the eater, so shall my word be that goes out from my mouth; it shall not return to me empty, but it shall accomplish that which I purpose, and shall succeed in the thing for which I sent it." God is present in this word of promise. Here we see that the prophet exhorts the exiles to trust God, who waters the land like a gardener and grows a harvest. They will buy wine and milk without money; they will eat good and rich food; they will call the nations, and the nations will come running; and they will be glorified.

The prophet says that when all of this happens, the mountains will sing and "the trees of the field shall clap their hands. Instead of the thorn shall come up the cypress; instead of the brier shall come up the myrtle; and it shall make a name for the Lord, and everlasting sign that shall not be cut off" (vv.12–13). Whereas Adam was sent out of the garden to work the ground only to produce thorns and thistles, Israel will be brought back to her garden and grow cypress and myrtle trees instead of thorns and briers.[53] Having served her exile-judgment, Israel will return to the land of milk and rich food—recalling the earlier description of Canaan as the land of milk and honey—to raise the name of her God as a sign to all people of His power. The fact that the people will know God's name and lift it up before the nations represents the climax of Adam's calling to name the animals in order to know God and, thus over time, to call Him by name in worship.

Not only will the trees clap their hands, but according to the psalmist, they also will joyously sing with all the earth in praise of God's anticipated future appearance and equitable judgment: "Let the heavens be glad, and let the earth rejoice; let the sea roar, and all that fills it; let the field exult, and everything in it! Then shall all the trees of the forest sing for joy before the Lord, for he comes, for he comes to judge the earth. He will judge the world in righteousness and the peoples in his faithfulness" (Ps. 96:11–13). The earth will break out with exuberance when God establishes proportion among His people. As noted above, proportionality is an integral dimension of the design of the first garden. God provides exactly what people need to live. Righteous judgment is proportional judgment in that it balances the needs of God's people with God's own satisfaction.

Isaiah connects the future of God's people with a garden of trees in other passages. For example, in 41:17–20, we read that God will "open rivers on the bare heights, and fountains in the midst of the valleys. [He] will make the wilderness a pool of water, and the dry land springs of water." This rejuvenation of the desert is followed by a list of trees that God will plant. "I will put in the wilderness the cedar, the acacia, the myrtle, and the olive. I will set in the desert the cypress, the plane and the pine together." We should note that it is the *Lord God* who will do this for Israel. "I the Lord will answer them; I the God of Israel will not forsake them." This corresponds to the story of the garden where it is the *Lord God* who channels rivers and plants trees. The turning of the wilderness into a flourishing garden promises a new chapter in God's creative activity. He will turn the place of judgment into one of blessing. The lesson we can take from what Isaiah writes to Israel in exile is that there are no situations— however barren, desolate, or hopeless—that God cannot renew. Whereas in the story of the Exodus, Canaan is a ready-made garden of milk and honey, here the garden is developed by God in the desert. More important, here the future garden is linked to the ministry of the servant of the Lord, who makes justice available to all people. By connecting the notion of justice to garden imagery, Isaiah wants people to see that it is an integral dimension of God's future for them.[54] According to the psalmist and Isaiah, the future garden of the people is a place of justice (*mišpat*) and righteousness (*zedeqah*). It is a place where the needs of people are recognized and met, and the requirements of God's covenant are honored.

The connection between justice and the garden is made again by Isaiah when he writes: "For the Lord comforts Zion; he comforts all her waste places and makes her wilderness like Eden, her desert like the garden of the Lord; joy and gladness will be found in her, thanksgiving and the voice of song." Joy and singing fill the future garden because the people all experience justice, and it is this justice that shines like a light to the nations. "My righteousness draws near, my salvation has gone out, and my arms will judge the peoples; the coastlands hope for me, and for my arm they wait" (Isa. 51:4–5). It cannot be said too often: like the Israelites before them, the exiles will be led to a land that is a garden from where they will lead the nations in worship and, now according to Isaiah, administer justice on their behalf.

Isaiah anticipates a land full of trees that will clap their hands when the people are resettled in God's presence. This response of jubilation is not simply due to the restoration of the people, but it is related to the purpose of God that all nations know and worship Him and experience justice. It is an expression that describes a return to inspiration, nourishment, enlightenment, and life by all of Adam's descendents. This prophecy long predates the Apostle Paul's perception that creation longs for the establishment of the sons of God and presently groans for God's purpose to be completed through them. He writes, "For the creation waits with eager longing for the revealing of the sons of God. For the creation was subjected to futility, not willingly, but because of him who subjected it, in hope that the creation itself will be set free from its bondage to decay and obtain the freedom of the glory of the children of God. For we know that the whole creation has been groaning together in the pains of childbirth until now" (Rom. 8:20–22). Paul could as well say that the trees are waiting to clap their hands. God did not place Adam in the garden to worship Him alone by tending to it, but He wants Adam to be a steward over all the living creatures of the earth. The celebratory nature of creation remains constrained apart from the naming activity of Adam.[55] Since his rebellion, all the earth has been waiting for its worship-leader to take his place once again and lead it in full praise and adoration of the Creator. When this happens, the trees of the fields will clap their hands in praise.

Isaiah envisions that this will happen when Israel returns to the land after her divinely imposed exile. In Paul's mind, however, the return to the garden already has begun with the life, death, and resurrection of Jesus, who he describes as the last Adam and who counters the disobedience of Adam with grace and obedience.[56] According to Paul, Jesus has already made a way of return to God.

Egypt and the Trees of Eden

The picture of the Garden of Eden as a grove of trees is retained by Ezekiel in his last lament against the nations.[57] In a long metaphorical passage, the exiled priest-turned-prophet compares Egypt to Assyria, which he says is like a cedar of Lebanon. Just as Assyria was a great power and yet was judged by God and overthrown by Babylon, so also Egypt will be brought low because of pride. Ezekiel begins by comparing Assyria's greatness to a well-watered tree with branches that provide protection for birds and animals. He says, "The cedars in the garden of God could not rival it, nor the fir trees equal its boughs; neither were the plane trees like its branches; no tree in the garden of God was its equal in beauty. I made it beautiful in the mass of its branches, and all the trees of Eden envied it that were in the garden of God" (Ezek. 31:8–9). This comparison emphasizes Assyria's glory. Despite its greatness, however, God judged her and her cut down. "And all the trees of Eden, the choice and best of Lebanon, all that drink water, were comforted in the world below" by this judgment. Ezekiel concludes by asking Egypt, "Who are you thus like in glory and in greatness among the trees of Eden? You shall be brought down with the trees of Eden to the world below. You shall be among the uncircumcised, with those who are slain by the sword" (Ezek. 31:16–18). If Assyria were a great cedar—the greatest tree of all trees, including those planted in the Garden of Eden—and was cut down, how does Egypt expect to escape judgment for her ways?

It is fascinating that the Garden of Eden continues to be the standard against which later reality—in this passage the reality of Egyptian pride and power in the late seventh to early sixth century—is interpreted. Though Isaiah anticipated a garden filled with trees that will one day rejoice and praise their Creator, Ezekiel prophesies about a well-watered plantation of trees that will judge Egypt for her wrongs. In both, the trees of the garden represent God's abundance, which, on the one hand, will be its own praise to God, and, on the other hand, will stand in judgment over the nations. All societies are measured by God's initial intention for Adam in the garden. The garden was designed as a place of obedience and faith in God's word as well as a place of rule and authority. This equilibrium of proportion is lost through arrogance and selfishness. It was lost to Adam for his rebellion, and the prophet says it will be lost to Egypt because of her pride. And it is lost to all of us when we live in our own autonomy and self-confidence.

The Fall of the King of Tyre

Prior to his lament over Egypt, Ezekiel pronounces woe upon the king of Tyre as part of his far-reaching judgment over all people at the time of Judah's exile. The fact that God had judged Judah for her sin did not mean that He intended to ignore the sins of others. After pronouncing judgment against Ammon, Moab, and Edom, he turns his attention westward to Tyre.[58] In his concluding oracle against the magnificent city-state, the prophet draws from the story of the garden to describe the egregious nature of the king and his city's way of life. The king is compared to an unnamed inhabitant of the garden who is surrounded by a hedge of precious stones and yet becomes proud and is thrown to the ground. More than likely this is an indirect reference to Adam, though some scholars think it is a veiled allusion to an angel.[59] What is clear is that he uses the story of the garden to discredit both king and city and to show the chasm that separates what was possible for Tyre (as was possible for Adam) with present reality due to sin. Tyre has committed "a multitude of iniquities" and gained wealth through "the unrighteousness of [his] trade" and for this he will be "turned to ashes" (Ezek. 28:18–19).

This passage is a lament; it is an expression not only of anger but also of sorrow. What better story to use than that of the Garden of Eden to express sorrow over the distorting effect of sin and pride on the grandeur of Tyre? Ezekiel says the king was "the signet of perfection"[60] and the image of wisdom and beauty. He was what God intended when He created man in His image were it not for his "lawless gain." Tyre exemplifies Adam, who attempted to achieve his own lawless gain by eating from the Tree of Knowledge despite God's prohibition. Here Tyre is a metaphor of lost possibility with God due to lawless behavior. Even though the king and city are Gentile, the prophet grieves over their loss. God has compassion for the nations.

But the garden, here, is also depicted as a place of purpose and of riches. Ezekiel says that the king has lived in the garden: "In Eden, the garden of God, you were, every precious stone your *hedge*: carnelian, peridot, and diamond, beryl, onyx, and jasper, sapphire, turquoise, and emerald; And of gold was the work of your tambours and settings, fixed in you on the day you were created."[61] This points to the garden God planted with trees, dug out channels for rivers, and filled with rare stones. The king is in the midst of a garden with a wall of precious stones all around him. However, one translation reads, "You were in Eden, the garden of God; every precious stone was your *covering*..." In this translation, the stones represent a cover instead of a hedge, like the breastplate worn by the high priest. It describes purpose and draws on the idea that Adam was appointed to be a priest in the garden to worship God. The king of Tyre is depicted as wearing precious stones like the priest that Adam was meant to be. Is Ezekiel envisioning a hedge of stones around the king as in the Garden of Eden, or does he see the king wearing a covering of stones like Israel's high priest, with an allusion to Adam as the first priest? Both ideas may be present in the passage, given Ezekiel's tendency to mix metaphors. Though *hedge* may be a better translation of the Hebrew, the listing of the precious stones undoubtedly recalls those in the high priest's breastplate[62] and points to the priestly role that Adam enjoyed. Regardless, Ezekiel would have surprised his audience by applying garden imagery to the king of Tyre. Yet should we expect anything less from someone who lay on his side for a year, cooked with human dung, envisioned a valley of skeletons, and imagined a new temple of extraordinary proportions? He draws on his creative knowledge to show how far Tyre has fallen. His fall is of mythical proportions and comparable only to that of Adam in the garden.

6

A Land of Wine: The Garden in the Prophets

Every Man under His Vine

In as much as Isaiah and Ezekiel recalled a garden of rivers and trees to describe Israel's future hope on the one hand, and what was lost on the other, other prophets focused on future hope and drew upon the picture of abundant wine to describe what this hope looked like. Since wine was one of the staples of the ancient Near Eastern diet known as the Mediterranean Triad, which also included oil and bread, it isn't unusual that the prophets regarded it as a sign of God's blessed future. The symbolic importance of wine dates to the wilderness story of the Exodus, when spies returned with large clusters of grapes after reconnoitering the land, proving the truth of God's promise.[63] The grapes, and the wine that would be produced from them, signified an abundant future for the people when all of their basic needs would be satisfied.[64]

Like his contemporary Isaiah, Micah draws upon garden imagery in his prophetic messages to the people of Judea in the eighth century. One passage in particular makes use of the garden to describe God's future work in their midst (4:1-5). In it, God speaks of the "latter days" when the nations will come to His mountain to learn His ways. At that time, He will judge them as they "beat their swords into ploughshares and their spears into pruning hooks." It is a time of peace when "[the nations] shall sit every man under his vine and under his fig tree." The future days envisioned by the prophet will be days when the produce of the vine and fig tree—wine and sweet foods—are consumed as people enjoy the rewards of their work. Weapons for fighting are forged into garden tools. The land will be a peaceful garden where God's people and the nations will rest secure in His presence and provision.

Fame Like the Wine of Lebanon

Another early prophet, Hosea, draws upon the imagery of the garden in his messages to the northern kingdom of Israel (chps. 9–10, 14). When he describes God's judgment for idolatry, he uses pictures like those used by Isaiah and Micah. God's punishment will be such that the "threshing floor and wine vat shall not feed them, and the new wine shall fail them. They shall not remain in the land of the Lord, but Ephraim shall return to Egypt." The people will be removed from the land of milk and honey to a place where "nettles shall possess their precious things of silver; thorns shall be in their tents." God will do to them what He did to Adam. The prophet goes on to compare Israel to a tree that has dried up and produces no fruit. Ironically, when Israel does produce fruit through God's blessing, the nation becomes proud: "Israel is a luxuriant vine that yields its fruit. The more his fruit increased, the more altars he built." Failure to fulfill their calling to be priests by worshipping the idols of other nations results in the removal of God's blessing and provision from them.

Nonetheless, God stands ready to take back His people and bless them. "I will heal their apostasy; I will love them freely, for my anger has turned from them. I will be like the dew to Israel; he shall blossom like the lily; he shall take root like the trees of Lebanon; his shoots shall spread out; his beauty shall be like the olive, and his fragrance like Lebanon. They shall return and dwell beneath my shadow; they shall flourish like the grain; they shall blossom like the vine; their fame shall be like the wine of Lebanon." In this beautiful, poetic passage, the prophet describes what God will do for His people upon their return. He will cause them to be a delightful, fragrant, and abundant garden. Yet the prophet does not envision a mere return to a garden; he sees the people transformed into a garden of trees, vines, flowers, and blossoms. Such will be the work of God as Israel's gardener that both their fame and His will go out among the nations. This means that Israel's testimony to the nations will be fulfilled when she returns to the covenant and receives God's blessing.

Faith without Wine

Later than Isaiah, Micah, and Hosea, Habakkuk delivers a prophetic message to the people of Judah and Jerusalem on the eve of the Babylonian conquest. It begins with the prophet's perplexity with the judgment of God. He knows that the people are deserving of judgment for idolatry, but why is God using the Babylonians to bring it about? After all, the proud and brutal men from Babylon are far more deserving of judgment than God's own people. God doesn't expect the prophet or the people to fully understand what He is doing: "For I am doing a work in your days that you would not believe if told" (Hab. 1:5). God knows who the Babylonians are and He expects the prophet and His people to trust His ways: "His soul [the Babylonians'] is puffed up; it is not upright within him, but the righteous shall live by his faith" (Hab. 2:4). God says to the prophet that faith is the proper response to His ways, as incomprehensible as they may seem. Faith is acceptance of and action in response to the word that God speaks given His faithfulness to them in the past. It is the attitude that Adam initially manifested in the garden and it is the attitude expected of Israel in Canaan. God had delivered their ancestors out of Egypt and given them a land flowing with milk and honey. Given that reality, they must now trust in His word concerning what He intends to do in the present.

That Habakkuk eventually responded to God's strong exhortation is seen in the concluding passage of the book. Like the earlier prophet Micah, Habakkuk concludes his message by declaring his faith in God and His ways, regardless of the circumstances in which he finds himself.

He asserts: "Though the fig tree should not blossom, nor fruit be on the vines, the produce of the olive fail and the fields yield no food, the flock be cut off from the fold and there be no herd in the stalls, yet I will rejoice in the Lord; I will take joy in the God of my salvation" (Hab. 3:17–18). With these stirring words, the prophet says that even when there is no evidence of the garden—when there are no figs for sweets, grapes for wine, olives for oil, produce to eat, livestock for milk and cheese—when there is no milk and honey—he will rejoice in God, whose ways and purposes are greater than he can fully understand. The prophet gives voice to a fresh understanding of the garden. For him, the garden of God is not seen in fields and fruit and folds but in the perfect will (purpose) of God performed among His people. This is why he can then say, "God, the Lord, is my strength." God's presence provides strength to Habakkuk and will give strength to the people in the most desperate situations as they trust in His ways. Habakkuk's God is strong and faithful, and His garden is one in which His will is fully accomplished.

A Land of Flowing Water and Sweet Wine

One of the most significant passages to describe the land after the time of exile is found in Ezekiel 40–48, which records the exiled priest's vision of a new temple, the return of the glory of God's presence to the temple, and the flow of water from the temple throughout the land, causing it to bloom with abundance. The fresh water will teem with fish, and all kinds of trees will grow along its shores, bearing fruit for healing (Ezek. 47:7–12). Of course, this vision recalls the original garden in terms of God's presence and provision while it anticipates the description of the New Jerusalem in Revelation 21–22.

This is not the only passage in Ezekiel that describes the land as a garden. The Lord says, "On the day that I cleanse you from all your iniquities, I will cause the cities to be inhabited, and the waste places shall be rebuilt. And the land that was desolate shall be tilled, instead of being the desolation that it was in the sight of all who passed by. And they will say, 'This land that was desolate has become like the Garden of Eden, and the waste and desolate and ruined cities are now fortified and inhabited.' Then the nations that are left all around you shall know that I am the Lord; I have rebuilt the ruined places and replanted that which was desolate. I am the Lord; I have spoken, and I will do it" (Ezek. 36:33–36). The prophet looks forward to a new garden that God will plant in a fallow and empty land.

This promise is followed by a vision of a valley littered with dry bones that are re-formed into living people by the Spirit (*ruah*) of God when Ezekiel prophesies to them (Ezek. 37:1–14). Together, these two passages show that a renewed land will be filled with renewed people through the restorative work of God's Spirit.[65] The prophet sees that the people have become defiled and deadened due to idolatry and are like unclean bones, which God will make clean by His Spirit so that they may once again live in His garden. Even as the Israelites had to be made clean before they entered Canaan—this was the purpose of the law of the covenant—so also the people in exile must be made clean before they can return to the replanted land of God's purpose. And that purpose is for God to be known and worshipped by all people.

The Mountains Will Drip Wine

Not only does Ezekiel see God's Spirit cleansing His people so they may once again inhabit a new garden, but the prophet Joel says that God will give His Spirit so that His people may fulfill His purposes in such a place. He declares that, in the day of the Lord, God will rejuvenate the land with rain and provide abundant produce for the people.[66] The result is that they will know "God is in the midst of Israel." This will be followed with an outpouring of God's Spirit so that His sons and daughters may prophesy. The prophet goes on to say that in the day of the Lord "the mountains shall drip sweet wine, and the hills shall flow with milk" (Joel 3:18), an allusion to "land flowing with milk and honey" in the Exodus story. This well-known passage describes a future day of God's presence with His people through His Spirit, His purpose for His people to prophesy, and His abundant provision of wine. Joel envisions a future garden in which the presence of the Lord is with the people in a new and personal way so that they may all speak His words with His help.

Both Ezekiel and Joel likely were inspired by the earlier prophet Amos, who spoke of a day when the land would "drip sweet wine and all the hills shall flow with it" and the people would plant on their land and build gardens (Amos 9:13–15). In these days, he says, "the plowman shall overtake the reaper and the treader of grapes him who sows seed." The days will be such that seedtime and harvest will merge together in productive work and super-abundant reward.

The ancient prophets of Israel and Judah expand the vision of the garden of God when they describe a future land full of wine. They teach us the truth that the garden is much more than a pleasant place free of worries. From Hosea, we learn that the people of God themselves will be a garden and their fame will be a witness to others of God's goodness; from Micah we learn that the garden is a place of peace and security where God's provision can be enjoyed by all; from Habakkuk we learn that the garden is a place of trust in God's purposes as mysterious as they may seem; from Ezekiel we learn that God will cleanse His people by His Spirit and replant them in a renewed land; and from Joel we learn that the garden is a place of God's presence by His Spirit where everyone has a part in His purposes.

7

Job's Hedge

If the prophets looked forward to a new garden where Israel will enjoy renewed relationship with God and abundant blessing in a way that recalls the Garden of Eden, the writer of the book of Job develops a riches-to-rags story about a man inside a hedge that recalls Adam and the first garden. Ultimately, the optimism of the writer for the future matches that of the prophets and is evident in Job's restoration at the end of the story. Whereas the prophets primarily anticipated the establishment of Israel in a future garden, the writer of Job envisions this for all people as represented in the person of Job.

Blameless Job

What kind of man is Job? From the beginning, he claims to be blameless (*tām*), a claim that the narrator seconds and God affirms in His remarks to Satan.[67] And before we wave away the notion that anyone, including Job, really can be blameless, we should keep in mind that Paul describes himself in this way to the Philippian believers when he asserts that he is "as to righteousness, under the law blameless" (Phil. 3:6). What does blameless mean, then, with respect to Job? Does it mean that he is perfect? More than likely it means that Job is a trustworthy servant of God within the hedge of His provision in a manner similar to Paul's trustworthiness as a servant of the Torah. He does what God tells him to do given the knowledge he has of God's word to him. So when God describes Job as "My servant" (*'abdî*), He describes him in a way that relates him to Adam, who worked (*'ābad*) in the garden. At the end of the story when Job repents, God again speaks of him as His servant.[68]

Though he is God's servant, Job's friends assert that he is still a sinner. Eliphaz, Bildad, and Zophar give Job the same advice: he must repent of the sin that is the cause of his suffering.[69] Yet throughout the story, Job maintains his innocence and says that he has not sinned.[70] His insistence on his innocence recalls Adam's remonstrance, "The woman whom you gave to be with me, she gave me fruit of the tree, and I ate" (Gen. 3:12). Given his newly-acquired knowledge from the tree, Adam attempts to exploit a technicality by pointing out that he didn't eat from the tree but only from the hand of the woman. Thus, he has not violated God's command by eating from the tree. The woman is to blame, or God, who gave the woman to him. Similarly, Job eventually declares that God is against him and responsible for his affliction. The irony is that both Adam and Job maintain their blamelessness after their encounter with the serpent/Satan, all the while denying the same to God. Adam does so by way of his newfound cleverness, Job by presuming greater knowledge than he actually possesses.

The Temptation of Job

Job's life is remarkable for the blessing that he enjoys. He has a large happy family, he has large healthy herds, and he offers sacrifices to God. He enjoys provision, has purpose, and experiences God's presence. God is pleased with Job and the life he lives. But Satan isn't convinced: "Does Job fear God for nothing?" He observes that Job is blessed and protected with a hedge around him. In this we see that Job lives in a special place of God's blessing reminiscent of Adam in the garden.

We do not want to miss the point in Satan's question. He disbelieves the claim that God makes about Job. God's word cannot be true. In the same manner, the serpent in the garden challenges the truthfulness of God's word. When the woman tells the creature that she is not permitted to eat from the Tree of Knowledge because it will result in her death, he replies, "You will not die," and he causes the woman herself to disbelieve the word that God has spoken to her.

Of course, the temptation with which the devil assaults Jesus in the wilderness represents a similar challenge to that thrown up by the serpent to the woman. At Jesus' baptism, a voice from heaven declares that he is the "beloved son." It is a divine declaration about Jesus' identity. Yet the devil challenges this affirmation and taunts him, "If you are the son of God ..." In effect, he says, "Are you God's son, really?" He attempts to sow doubt in Jesus' mind about his identity and urges that he prove it.[71]

Job succumbs to the affliction Satan brings against him and holds God accountable for his sad and tragic circumstance. He follows the example of Adam, who says that God is responsible for his predicament: "The woman whom you gave to be with me, she gave me fruit of the tree, and I ate." This is how we all respond to hard circumstances or failure. We shift blame and often accuse God. Yet Job is in no position to place judgment on God's ways. After God speaks to him out of the storm-wind, Job relents and accepts His word. He is confronted with the God of creation who is also the God of the hedge. Where was Job at creation? Where was he when God built His hedge? The question reminds him that he is finite and cannot know all things apart from God. Ultimately, Job repents for his presumption to know more than he does. Such repentance—which for Job is a turning to a new way of thinking about God—leads to renewed blessing in his life.[72]

Knowing Good and Evil

Job's friends are godly counselors. They mourn with him and they respond to his predicament with singular advice: Job must repent for his sin. Eliphaz believes that people bring on their own trouble through sin, Bildad believes that Job needs forgiveness for sin, and Zophar believes that Job deserves greater punishment for his sin than what he has received.[73] They claim to know the answer to Job's dilemma and in this way they presume to know "good and evil."[74] The fact is that Job's friends are right when they say that he is a sinner even as Job is right when he says that he is blameless. They are also wrong.

Only God knows all things and only He knows the source of Job's affliction. Thus, the conflict between Job and his friends is the result of thinking that they know more than they really do.

The restitution to Job of what he has lost anticipates the future restoration to Adam of his original position before God. God's servant Job regains both his position and his possessions when he confesses, "I know you can do all things" and "I have uttered what I did not understand" (Job 42:2–3). This calls to mind Jesus' declaration that "with man this is impossible, but with God all things are possible" in reference to the obstacles that rich people like Job face in entering God's kingdom (Matt. 19:26). Job's confession of his own ignorance reveals that he has learned that he does not know all things. In his humility before God and newfound knowledge of Him, Job once again receives the blessing of God in his life. In essence, he has eschewed Adam's presumption to eat from the Tree of Knowledge. Job initially imagined that he knew all things, but through God's revelation of himself, he sees that he doesn't. The last chapter of the book, therefore, serves as a guide for the entire story. The story of Job is about all of us who are created to live with integrity in the garden and yet are not identical to our Creator. It reminds us that we have been created for a garden—within the hedge of God's blessing and protection—in order to know God. Not to presume knowledge of all things as did Job, but to know God. Just as Adam was placed in the garden for this purpose, so also was Job, and so also are we.

8

Jesus and the Garden

Jesus in the Wilderness

As we have noted several times, God was present in the garden with Adam by speaking His word to him and by drawing near to have fellowship with him. He provided everything that Adam needed to live and prosper by planting trees in the garden. In addition, He gave purpose to Adam by making him responsible for tending and keeping the garden like a priest and for naming the animals. When Adam ate the fruit of the Tree of Knowledge and disobeyed God's word, he not only brought death upon himself but he also inhibited the created world from experiencing its own fulfillment. Paul writes, "For we know that the whole creation has been groaning together in the pains of childbirth until now"

(Rom. 8:22). How could Adam's action not have affected the world? He was the priest of creation and what he did impacted what God had entrusted to his care. The death of Adam and the constriction of creation began with his disobedience and banishment from the garden.

The image of the wilderness is descriptive of Adam's home after his banishment. It is a place of thorns and thistles, sweat and pain, curses and death. It is the place where blood is spilled and alienation becomes his natural condition. It is into such a wilderness that the Spirit propels Jesus upon his baptism. Whereas Adam received the life-breath of God and began his life in the garden, Jesus receives the Spirit and is immediately pushed into the wilderness. It is important to see that Jesus begins his ministry in Adam's exile. He initiates his ministry of restoration in the place of Adam's desolation. The Gospels are unanimous in recounting Jesus' temptation in the wilderness as the first move in the overthrow of the effects of Adam's disobedience in the Garden of Eden.

There are three parts to the wilderness temptation. First, Jesus is tempted to prove his identity and provide for his own needs. The devil says he should turn stones into loaves of bread and provide for himself and thereby show that he is indeed God's son. After all, didn't God provide everything Adam needed to live in the garden? Didn't He give manna to Israel in the wilderness? Jesus is tempted to use the Spirit to serve his own needs, even though God gives His Spirit so he can serve the needs of others. The second temptation is like the first, this time at the temple where God's Messiah was expected to appear in glory one day. He is tempted to prove God's presence with him through a demonstration of angelic power. Whereas the first temptation urged Jesus to reprise Israel's miracle provision in the desert, the second temptation prods him to inaugurate Israel's future miracle of God's presence in the Messiah. Third, Jesus is tempted to accomplish God's purpose, which is to gain the kingdoms of the earth for his Father, through his own means. If he won't call upon the Spirit to meet his own needs and if he won't call upon God's messengers to convince temple leaders and the people of the veracity of his ministry, then let him act on his own initiative to do what God wants. If Jesus bows down to the devil, he will win the nations. He will accomplish God's purpose in a fast, efficient, and effortless way. The third temptation asks, "Why go the way of submission? Why not achieve God's goal through a different means?" Taken together, these three temptations represent the devil's effort to block the planting of a new garden of provision, presence, and purpose.

The third temptation is decisive. God gave Adam a command and then He gave him responsibility to name the animals. As we have seen, the naming of animals is not a type of parlor game as we might think of it. God was establishing the means by which Adam would learn about the created world and about his Creator. Through observation, reflection, and description, Adam would grow in his knowledge about the things that God had brought into existence. God's plan was that over time, with careful, precise, and strenuous effort, Adam's knowledge of God's good creation and of God himself would grow. The serpent interfered with this plan by tempting Adam to take the way of convenience—Adam was tempted to eat from the tree and gain such understanding without the submission and discipline involved in God's way.

The serpent deceived the woman by telling her the truth ("When you eat of [the tree] your eyes will be opened and you will be like God, knowing good and evil"), all the while encouraging her to follow a way other than that set by God for gaining such truth. He tempted her to take the easy way.

The devil tempts Jesus to take a short cut as well. He motions for him to leave the road that will eventually pass through Golgotha and go beyond to glory. He will give the kingdoms of the world to Jesus if Jesus the king will worship him. Of course he will. If the king of the kingdoms will submit to him, then the devil will have final authority over the kingdoms. The devil gained authority in the world when Adam abdicated his own authority by submitting to the word of the serpent. Now he attempts to keep Jesus from regaining Adam's authority by having him submit to his word rather than the one spoken to him by his Father at Jordan: "You are my beloved son."

After his temptation in the wilderness, Jesus returns to Galilee, where he says, "The time is fulfilled, and the kingdom of God is at hand; repent and believe in the gospel" (Mark 1:15). By saying that the kingdom was present, Jesus was saying that the day of reentry into the garden of God had begun, where people could experience God's presence and find full provision for their lives as they lived out His purpose to be His image by following his example. The way into the garden was wide open, and people were free to enter into it as long as they were willing to go through the gate of God's word, exemplified in His son (John 10:1–18).

The Advance of the Kingdom

Adam's role in the earth as one made in God's image was to increase so God's image might also increase and shine forth. He was to do this from within the garden, where he was given provision, understood his purpose, and experienced God's presence. Another way of saying this is that he was given the task (purpose) of realizing the possibilities of the created world on behalf of his Creator by working with the form, order, and diversity of that world (provision) and growing the garden in the rest of creation so that the presence of God was known everywhere.

But Jesus doesn't speak in this way to his disciples and the crowds. Instead, he speaks of the kingdom of God. The importance of the kingdom in Jesus' thinking is evident in that it is the first thing he addresses upon his return from the wilderness after his baptism. He declares, "The time is fulfilled, and the kingdom of God is at hand; repent and believe in the gospel" (Mark 1:15). Moreover, it is one of the last things on his mind before his crucifixion. When Pilate asks Jesus if he is a king, Jesus acknowledges that he is such but that his kingdom is unlike anything Pilate can imagine (John 18:33–38). And after the resurrection, Jesus continues to teach the disciples about the kingdom as they wonder if he will now establish it in their midst (Acts 1:6–8). Their question makes sense given that when they asked Jesus how they should pray, he drew their attention to the kingdom. "Pray then like this: 'Our Father in heaven, hallowed be your name. Your kingdom come, your will be done, on earth as it is in heaven" (Matt. 6:9–10). The disciples are to have the coming of the kingdom on their minds as they pray. The importance of this is that it joins their thoughts to the yearning of the Spirit, who John says is presently calling, "Come, Lord Jesus" (Rev. 22:17). The last book of the New Testament concludes with the hopeful request that the enthroned Jesus will return and fully establish God's kingdom.

Not only is the kingdom present in the ministry of Jesus but it is advancing forward. This is as it should be since the garden was to grow under the care of Adam. When disciples of John the Baptist approach Jesus and ask if he is the Messiah, they are asking if he is the coming king. John is uncertain since Jesus has not made any effort to seize authority in Jerusalem and expel the Romans. Jesus responds by pointing to the effects of his ministry and teaching. He identifies the kingdom of the Messiah with healing, restoration, and good news. "Go and tell John what you hear and see; the blind receive their sight and the lame walk, lepers are cleansed and the deaf hear, and the dead are raised up, and the poor have good news preached to them" (Matt. 11:4–5). Then he says that the kingdom has been coming violently: "From the days of John the Baptist until now the kingdom of heaven has been coming violently and the violent take it by force."[75] It has been advancing with violence by overthrowing the works of darkness. Blindness is dispelled, deafness is penetrated, the weak are strengthened, impurity is cleansed, death is defeated, and good news is broadcast over despair and hopelessness. By saying that the kingdom was advancing violently, Jesus was saying that the garden was growing and that the place of God's presence, purpose, and provision was expanding.

This advance is also evident in the so-called nature miracles performed by Jesus.[76] Examples of these include the stilling of the sea, walking on water, and the feeding of five thousand men. Sometimes these miracles are interpreted as acts of magic. More often, they are dismissed altogether. Instead, they should be viewed as signs of Adam's dominion over the created world through Jesus and the enablement of that world to praise God by assisting in His purposes through His son. Thus, when Jesus commands the winds to calm and when he walks on the sea, he is ordering creation once again to serve the purposes of God that are now being achieved in him and require that he reach the disciples to continue his ministry among them.[77]

The feeding of five thousand men deserves special comment since it is the only miracle recorded in all four Gospels. It is often interpreted as a sign of a future heavenly banquet that God will provide for His people. He shows in a partial way what will be complete in the future. Though this is no doubt true, the miracle also points back to the provision God made for Adam. When Jesus provides food for five thousand men, he establishes a virtual garden for the people. The abundant provision of loaves and fish draws their attention to his teaching about the kingdom of God that he says is now present. And by calling people to respond to the kingdom in his ministry, Jesus is challenging them to think in a new way about God's purpose for them as sons and daughters of God. This creation miracle is but a small indication of the service that God intends for His created world to have in His kingdom.

As one who has the Spirit of God, Jesus enjoys the immediate presence of God in his life to provide for the needs of the people and instruct them about their purpose, which is to live as men and women of an advancing kingdom. Though they may look to the past garden for insight into the present, the kingdom goes before them and they must look forward to the new garden envisioned by the prophets, now being revealed in Jesus' ministry. All of these miracles are signs that the trees of the hills have begun to clap their hands at the presence of Jesus, who performs God's purposes by the power of God's Spirit.

Garden Lessons in the Teaching of Jesus

In the Sermon on the Mount, Matthew records Jesus saying, "Look at the birds of the air; they neither sow nor reap nor gather into barns, and yet your heavenly Father feeds them. Are you not of more value than they?" (Matt. 6:26) This is garden theology at its best. Jesus sees in the created world a lesson about the nature of God: He is the Creator who provides for all of His creatures and especially for His people, given His grand plans for them. God is the Father who has a personal interest in His creation and cares for the smallest of that creation (the birds) as well as the greatest (the disciples). Jesus is able to make this observation because he has seen in the created world a revelation of God himself.

Jesus continues by saying, "Consider the lilies of the field, how they grow: they neither toil nor spin, yet I tell you, even Solomon in all his glory was not arrayed like one of these. But if God so clothes the grass of the field, which today is alive and tomorrow is thrown into the oven, will he not much more clothe you" (Matt. 6:28–30). Again, Jesus looks to the created world and sees a garden truth: God has provided for His people—here the disciples—so they may fulfill His purposes for their lives. They are not to worry about their daily needs but devote themselves to the divine purposes of God. What Jesus says here is not a casual comment based on a passing observation of nature. Rather, it is an astute insight into the nature of God through His created order that has come about by the Spirit's revelation.

These examples are important in that they reveal a primary way in which Jesus reprises Adam's original role. Adam was created to exercise dominion over God's created world and given the opportunity to learn about God through that world by naming the animals. By choosing to eat of the Tree of Knowledge, he chose to learn about God in another way, which is no way at all. God had intended Adam to learn about Him through careful observation of the world in which he had been placed, with the very life of God's Spirit in him and by giving attention to His word. Jesus' observation of the birds of the air and the lilies of the field, and his precise understanding of human behavior and everyday life, as evident in his parables, complements his profound knowledge of and submission to God's word and shows that he lives in the manner that God intended for Adam.

The Garden in the Parable of the Prodigal Son

Not only was Jesus a student of the natural world around him, he was also a student of human nature.

His profound understanding of men and women is evident in his stories about good Samaritans and fearful priests, shrewd managers, banquet hosts, cost-counting contractors, barn-building land owners, seed-scattering farmers, persistent widows, and diligent shepherds. It is certainly evident in the story of the prodigal son, which may be the best-known of all his parables (Luke 15:11–32). Though the parable certainly is about God's love for His people as depicted by a loving father's welcome of a wayward son, at a universal level it is a story about estrangement and reconciliation. According to Geraint Vaughn Jones, it is about human freedom, decision, alienation, and restoration. He writes, "When the Prodigal walks out of his father's house, and when Adam leaves the Garden of Eden, they enter a disenchanted world in which they are not at home."[78] The story Jesus tells has resonated with hearers for centuries because it describes our common experience. At home, the son enjoyed the presence of his father, the provision of his house, and the purpose in being an heir of his household. Yet he eschews these blessings for an immediate inheritance and a self-indulgent way of life. Like Adam, the prodigal chooses not to wait for his inheritance. He wants it now and acts to gain what he wants without the patience and discipline of obedience.

The son finds himself in a distant country, hungry and feeding pigs. He doesn't have enough to eat, doesn't have purpose for his life, and is far away from his father. Jesus says that he "came to himself" and makes his way back to his father and his home. He is like Adam, who must work by the sweat of his brow in an alien place without the purpose given to him by God. His energy and effort is not directed to naming animals and learning about the Creator but on feeding pigs and providing for his own needs from corncobs and husks. The prodigal realizes that the way of his father is far better than the way he has chosen—he comes to himself. In telling the story, Jesus invites everyone to come to themselves by choosing the way that he has modeled. The invitation is to return to the garden.

The Garden of God's Will

The father's house is a better place indeed, but getting there is not always easy. As biblical scholar Kenneth Bailey points out, there would be village residents to pass through who likely would perform a kezazah ceremony and ban him from returning.[79] So how is the prodigal, or any of us for that matter, able to get back to the father's house? It is to follow Jesus through the Garden of Gethsemane. At first glance, Gethsemane appears to be the antitype of the Garden of Eden. It is a place of blood-beaded sweat, anguish, and unfulfilled personal desire compared to Eden's plenitude, purpose, and promise. So, how is Gethsemane like the first garden in any way? Matthew reports that the night before his crucifixion, Jesus takes Peter, James, and John away from the others to watch with him. Then he prays, "My Father, if it be possible, let this cup pass from me; nevertheless, not as I will, but as you will" (Matt. 26:36–39). Three times he prays this prayer and grapples with submission, obedience, and the purpose of his life and ministry. Jesus intends the disciples to watch (*grēgoreō*) with him; he does not intend for them only to keep him company, but he wants them to be witnesses of his devotion to God's purpose. Jesus wants them to see that garden life involves obedience to God's will that at times is desperately and agonizingly hard.

By declaring such devotion, Jesus commits to the purpose of God with his words, and by acknowledging his identity to the soldiers when they come with torches and swords, he commits to God's will with his actions. He doesn't flee and hide. But Gethsemane is not only a place of purpose for Jesus; it is also a place of God's presence. This is evident when Jesus calls to God as *Father*. He doesn't call upon a higher power or cry out to God as King of the Universe, Maker of Heaven and Earth, or Master of Creation. He calls upon "my Father," and by naming God as Father he reveals an intimacy with God that speaks of presence. [80] He is not alone in the garden. He is in the presence of the one who loves him.

If we see purpose and presence in Gethsemane, is it possible that there is provision there as well? No provision is described, yet we want to know how Jesus commits to the purpose of his Father in this ominous and iron-heavy hour. How can Jesus say, "The hour is at hand, and the Son of Man is betrayed into the hands of sinners. Rise, let us be going; see, my betrayer is at hand," without running away into the night? What provision does he draw upon? We find the answer in the book of Hebrews, where the writer describes the redemption provided by Jesus' shed blood. He observes, "For if the sprinkling of defiled persons with the blood of goats and bulls and with the ashes of a heifer sanctifies for the purification of the flesh, how much more will the blood of Christ, who through the eternal Spirit offered himself without blemish to God, purify our conscience from dead works to serve the living God" (Heb. 9:13–14). This passage reveals that

Jesus was enabled by the Spirit of God to give himself as a sacrifice for human need. The provision upon which Jesus draws to give his life on behalf of others so that they might live to God is none other than God's Spirit. It is the same provision that he has drawn upon throughout his ministry. Through his submission to his Father's will that he bear his cross with the help of the Spirit, Jesus provides abundant life for those who join their lives to his (John 10:10).

Moreover, when Jesus prays, "Father, your will be done," he prays the same prayer he has already taught his disciples and us to pray. In that prayer, Jesus encourages us to direct our prayers to our "Father in heaven." We are to view God as personal, like a father, even as we recognize Him as transcendent and great in His holiness. As a father, God desires to provide for His children; as one who abides in heaven, He possesses the power and means to fulfill that desire.

In the Lord's Prayer, we also are taught to pray that God's kingdom come upon the earth in our lives as it is in heaven, which is equivalent to asking that His will and rule be established over us. Once we acknowledge God as immanent and transcendent, personal and powerful, we can request that His will be accomplished in our lives because we know the one from whom we ask. Otherwise, we would be asking for something that we can't conceive or achieve. With this in mind we are to ask for provision in order to fulfill God's purpose. The prayer reminds us that we cannot accomplish God's will—we cannot see the kingdom manifested in our lives—with our own resources. We do not possess the desire, knowledge, or strength to see God's will done; we need His understanding and power to do what He wants. Therefore, we ask for daily bread. We ask for God's will to be done here (on earth as it is in heaven) and now (daily bread).

The prayer goes on to reveal that God's will is for us to live in the way of forgiveness and reconciliation since this is the most basic expression of proportionality for our lives. It is that we experience reconciliation with each other as we have with Him and be rejoined to our place in the world of creation. With God's provision of daily bread and forgiveness, we are to forgive one another and live out His will. We also pray for protection from ourselves—temptation to live in a way apart from God's word and the forgiveness that should distinguish our lives—and from the evil one who wants to steal our identity as sons and daughters of God, kill the life that God provides for us, and destroy God's ambitious plans for us (John 10:10).

When Jesus commits to the will of his Father in the garden, he fulfills the purpose that God originally had for Adam. He commits to obedience. He also commits to forgiveness and asks his Father to forgive those who have rejected his message, held him up to ridicule, and brutally nailed him to a tree. Forgive them for their ignorance, he prays (Luke 23:34), and in this he shows the way to knowledge and relationship with God and one another that was lost through disobedience. He makes this commitment through the strength of the Spirit, confident that his Father hears him because He is with him. Jesus' garden prayer—God's will be done—is to be our prayer as well. When we pray this prayer and live by its truth with the help of the Spirit and aware of God's great purpose, we set ourselves in the garden with him.

The Promise of Paradise

Not only does Jesus transform Gethsemane into the Garden of Eden with his declaration of fidelity to God's will, but also he anticipates the garden at Golgotha. Luke shows how, hoisted between two violent men (*lēstai*) outside the city walls, Jesus finds himself in the same existential wilderness as the one at the beginning of his ministry (23:32–43). Abandoned and alone, Jesus is again tempted by the devil, this time through the taunts of the soldiers: "If you are the king of the Jews, save yourself!" He can end his misery and prove his royalty in one great self-serving act. It's not too late. While one thief joins the people and soldiers in mocking him, the other asks for mercy: "Jesus, remember me when you come into your kingdom." Jesus says that he will be with him in paradise. The Greek word is *paradeisos*, the same word used to translate *garden* in Genesis 2. When Jesus asserts, "Today you will be with me in paradise," he says to the condemned man, in essence, "Today you will join me in the garden of God's presence, purpose, and provision."

Jesus' promise to the thief is the *paradeisos* of presence—"you will be *with me.*" Jesus does not speak of a future paradise park but of his presence. In a real sense, the thief has already entered into the garden. Howard Hageman is prescient when he says, "To be with Jesus Christ, whenever and wherever it takes place, is to be in paradise."[81] Though there is a future reality to paradise, that reality has entered into our existence here and now. This is why Hageman also says that there is "no paradise possible in another world for those who have not begun, however imperfectly, their experience of it here."[82] There is no more imperfect place to begin the experience of the garden than on an ugly, dirty, bloody Roman cross. And yet it is there that the thief hears the promise of the garden from Jesus: "Today you will be with me in paradise."

The Resurrected Gardener

Early on the morning of the first day of the week after Jesus' execution, Mary Magdalene went to the tomb to anoint his dead body. There in the dawn, she mistakenly identified the resurrected Jesus as the local gardener. "She turned around and saw Jesus standing, but she did not know that it was Jesus … Supposing him to be the gardener, she said to him, 'Sir, if you have carried him away, tell me where you have laid him" (John 20:14–15). Though Mary did not recognize Jesus at first, she was right to think of him as a gardener. Only, Jesus is not the caretaker of a burial ground but the gardener of God's eternal and living presence.

Jesus fulfills all of the requirements of the first gardener, Adam, and transforms this place of death into one of life even as he transformed Gethsemane and Golgotha into gardens like the one present in Eden. He cultivates provision and purpose when he goes to his disciples, breathes on them, and says, "Receive the Holy Spirit. If you forgive the sins of anyone, they are forgiven; if you withhold forgiveness from anyone, it is withheld" (John 20:23). All that they will need to live as his disciples and fulfill his commandment to love through forgiveness is provided by the Spirit. It is the Spirit who provides the authority, discernment, and humility to forgive, which is the first and most fundamental ministry of those who follow Jesus. The authority to forgive rests with God, who gives His Spirit so the disciples may exercise His right. The discernment to forgive also rests with God, for who knows when there is genuine repentance other than God? The Spirit enables Jesus' disciples to distinguish true repentance from self-serving dissembling behavior. And the humility to forgive originates with God and the sacrifice of His son. Only the Spirit can give the power needed to ask for forgiveness and to accept it when offered. This is the purpose that God has granted to His people. Later, the apostle Paul will write to the church at Corinth that everyone in Christ is "a new creation." To them he says, "All this is from God, who through Christ reconciled us to himself and gave us the ministry of reconciliation; that is, in Christ God was reconciling the world to himself, not counting their trespasses against them, and entrusting to us the message of reconciliation" (2 Cor. 5:17–19). The new purpose of reconciliation is given to all of us who have become a new creation by the power of God through Jesus, the resurrected gardener.

9

Paul's Experience of the Garden

The Fruit of the Spirit

To be a new creation is to be a person who is like the trees of the garden that are laden with fruit. Paul writes about the fruit of the Spirit in his letter to the Galatians, where he exhorts Gentile believers to use the freedom they have been given in Christ not to serve themselves and do what they want but to serve others. Such a use of freedom to "love your neighbor as yourself" fulfills "the whole law." This recalls Jesus' teaching in the Sermon on the Mount when he declares, "So whatever you wish that others would do to you, do also to them, for this is the Law and the Prophets" (Matt. 7:12). At another time, Jesus responds to a scribe by saying, "The most important [commandment] is, 'Hear, O Israel: The Lord our God, the

Lord is one. And you shall love the Lord your God with all your heart …' The Second is this: 'You shall love your neighbor as yourself'" (Mark 12:29–31).

Paul elaborates on this exhortation by contrasting the life of self-centered freedom, which he calls the flesh (Gal. 5:19–21) with the life of inclusive freedom, which he describes as Spirit-cultivated fruit (Gal. 5:22–23). Freedom of the flesh serves one's own wants and desires. The behavior listed by Paul describes life lived in pursuit of excitement, gratification, and self-interest. It is life lived in a personal pleasure park. There is no regard for others in such living. People in the flesh give no thought to service. People who live to please the flesh, Paul says, "will not inherit the kingdom of God" (Gal. 5:21). In other words, such people will not find their way back to the garden. This is because they follow the same way of self-centered freedom that resulted in Adam's expulsion from the garden in the first place. We are told that after the serpent enticed Eve, she saw that the tree seemed good to eat, was beautiful to behold, and offered a means for obtaining wisdom apart from the way established by God. It offered everything but relationship with God. Even so, she wanted the fruit of the tree. The Galatians are to resist the way of the flesh and, instead, follow the way of the Spirit and desire the fruit the Spirit gives. When they do this, they will inherit God's kingdom and make their way into the garden of God.

God cultivates fruit in our lives by His Spirit so that we may strengthen and nourish each other. The fruit of the Spirit described by Paul includes love, joy, peace, patience, kindness, goodness, faithfulness, gentleness, and self-control (Gal. 5:22–23). To use our freedom to walk in the way of the Spirit so that such fruit may be grown in our lives is to fulfill the command of Jesus and show ourselves to be his disciples. Who benefits from the fruit that the Spirit grows in our lives? Others do. Family members, neighbors, people at work, and those in the church eat the fruit that the Spirit grows in us and are nourished by it. When we show patience toward our loved ones, for example, we help them learn and grow in their lives. When we are faithful toward other people, we engender confidence in them toward us. When we reach out to neighbors in peace, they are joined to us in relationship. When we act in kindness toward fellow church members, we bless them and show that they are understood. The fruit of the Spirit is the primary way by which God's people are strengthened and enabled to reflect God's image and do His will.

Paul concludes his teaching in this passage with the same point that he made in the introduction: Jesus has given freedom to us so that we might love and serve others. He writes, "Bear one another's burdens, and so fulfill the law of Christ" (Gal. 6:2). The law of Christ is not a general reference to all of Jesus' teaching such as that given in the Sermon on the Mount. Specifically, it is the commandment that Jesus gives to the disciples the night before his crucifixion, according to John: "A new commandment I give to you, that you love one another: just as I have loved you, you also are to love one another. By this all people will know that you are my disciples, if you have love for one another."[83] This new commandment or law that Jesus gives is so important that he repeats it to the disciples several times afterward. For example, he says to the disciples later, "If you love me, you will keep

my commandments ... Whoever has my commandments
and keeps them, he it is who loves me ... If anyone loves
me, he will keep my word" (John 14:15, 21, 23). Jesus is
speaking of the commandment to love each other, which
he has modeled for them by washing their feet. Even later,
he says, "If you keep my commandments, you will abide
in my love ... This is my commandment, that you love one
another as I have loved you ... These things I command
you, so that you will love one another" (John 15:10, 12,
17). For love to be meaningful, it must be practical, which
is why Jesus says that he will send the Spirit to be with
them. The disciples will only be able to love each other
in the way that Jesus has demonstrated with the help of
the Spirit. It is beyond them otherwise.[84] In teaching the
disciples his law of love, Jesus says that he is the vine and
they are the branches and that they have been created to
bear fruit. In the context of the passage, it is clear that they
will bear fruit with the help of the Spirit. For this reason,
God prunes them so they may bear as much as possible:
"By this my Father is glorified, that you bear much fruit
and so prove to be my disciples" (John 15:1–8).

Paul draws upon this teaching, which is why he says
that to love is to help one another. It is to share in their
lives in such a way that makes their life easier. Simply
put, he says that it is to do good things to others. "Let
us not grow weary of doing good (things), for in due
season we will reap, if we do not give up. So then, as we
have opportunity, let us do good (things) to everyone, and
especially to those who are of the household of faith" (Gal.
6:9–10). Paul says that we have been given freedom to love
one another. We are enabled to do this by the Spirit, who
grows fruit in our lives for the benefit of others. When we

walk in the Spirit and bear fruit in our lives, we lift the burdens of others and do good things for them.

Paul is not the only New Testament writer to write about the fruit of the Spirit. Peter does so too, though he does not describe it in the same way that Paul does. In his second letter, he exhorts his people to participate in God's divine nature through God's divine power (2 Pet. 1:3–4). These characteristics are remarkably similar to the fruit of the Spirit identified by Paul in Galatians, and include virtue, knowledge, self-control, perseverance, godliness, brotherly kindness, and love. What Paul identifies as divine fruit, Peter describes as the divine nature. For both apostles, these characteristics reflect the very life of God in the follower of the Lord Jesus. That Peter is thinking in the same way as Paul is revealed in his claim that such characteristics will keep one from being "unfruitful" (2 Pet. 1:8).

Peter says the result of developing the divine nature in one's life is "entrance into the eternal kingdom of our Lord and Savior Jesus Christ" (2 Pet. 1:11) which compares to Paul's assertion that fruit of the Spirit leads to eternal life. Furthermore, he says that it is the opposite of sinful desire, which again recalls Paul's comparison between the life of the Spirit and that of the flesh. Peter's "eternal kingdom" and Paul's "eternal life" both point to the garden of God, where He is present to cultivate His nature or fruit in the lives of His people.

The Spirit grows fruit in the lives of the followers of Jesus for service. Since this fruit represents the very nature of God, according to Peter, the Spirit enables us to manifest God's presence and provision to each other as we live in relationship with one another. This resembles the original purpose for which Adam was made as well as the provision that God made for him in the garden. Adam was created to be God's image in the earth and to serve as a priest in God's created world. In addition, God gave him what he needed to reflect His image and carry out his priestly duties. The fruit trees of the garden represent this provision. But God did not only provide for Adam's physical needs; He also provided for his spiritual, emotional, and aesthetic needs. What was the spiritual and emotional provision that God made for Adam? Certainly it included love, joy, peace, patience, kindness, goodness, faithfulness, gentleness, and self-control. These qualities are given by the Spirit and thus represent divine attributes that God intended Adam to manifest as His image on the earth. They were and are essential for human beings to reflect God's nature in the creation.

The way in which the fruit of the Spirit relates to the divine presence, abundant provision, and meaningful purpose of the garden may be briefly summarized. Beginning with joy, (1) it is the natural response to God's presence and the fulfillment of His purpose. (2) Peace is oneness with God's presence and purpose and the embrace of relationship with Him and His people. (3) Patience is trust in the order of God's purpose among His people. (4) Kindness is support for others in the fulfillment of God's purpose. (5) Goodness is the practical expression of God's purpose and presence toward others.[85] (6) Faithfulness is commitment to God's purpose with the provision He gives. (7) Gentleness is sensitivity to God's presence and the way and manner of His purpose in the lives of others. (8) Self-control is submission to God's order and purpose and acceptance of the provision He gives for it to be accomplished. When God's people obey His word and align their desires with His so that His might be fulfilled in their lives, they manifest self-control and a repudiation of the desires of the flesh. (9) Of course, the first of the fruit listed by Paul is love, which he defines at length in his letter to the Corinthian church as the perfect example of inclusive freedom (1 Cor. 13).

In sum, the imagery of the church as a grove of fruit-bearing trees suggests that in Paul's mind, the garden is to some extent present in the life of God's people. It recalls the vision of Hosea and that of the psalmist, who saw Israel as a vine or tree in the midst of the garden (Hos. 14; Ps. 80). The Spirit grows fruit in order to help us be God's image in the world: a people who are joyful, peaceful, patient, kind, good, faithful, gentle, and submitted to His purposes are fulfilling their priestly duties before Him even as they manifest His presence in the world. Simply stated, as the Spirit grows divine fruit in our lives, the garden of God is recreated in our midst.

The Gifts of the Garden

The Spirit gives gifts to God's people as well. God not only gave Adam what he needed to be His image and reflect His character in the earth, He also provided him with the abilities to tend, protect, and cultivate the garden, as well as to exercise dominion over the creatures of the earth. Paul views the gifts of God in the same way that he does the fruit of the Spirit. Both are a vital part of the life of God's people. Just as the fruit is given for the benefit of others so God's image may be manifested among them, so too the gifts are given to enable them to carry out their priestly duties. The gifts are given to people for people and are oftentimes the people themselves. Thus, Paul intimates that apostles, prophets, evangelists, pastors, and teachers are gifts or blessings given to God's people to form them into the body of Christ (Eph. 4:11–12). He says that these people-gifts are given to others so they may grow into the fullness of Christ and not be hindered by empty teachings, human speculations, or deceitful schemes (Eph. 4:14). The allusion to Adam in the garden here shows that Paul sees these gifts as a primary way the church is prepared to resist false teaching and deceitful arguments, such as Adam experienced in the garden, and become like Christ, who is, in essence, the image of God (Col. 1:15–20).

In addition to these people-gifts, Paul writes about words-gifts and abilities (*charismata*) that God gives so His people may act as Christ in the world (1 Cor. 12:4–11). Since a gift is given or a favor granted at the discretion of the one who gives it, those described by Paul here emphasize God's desire for His people. Together they reflect blessings of the garden that enable God's people to accomplish His purposes. As Allen Ross observes, "[The] garden was to be the one place in the world where all the beautiful and beneficial gifts of God were concentrated."[86] It is evident from those Paul lists that God desires His people to be endowed with wisdom, understanding, trust, wholeness, and power. He wants them to be able to name and discern the truth and reality of His creation and to speak to Him from within the creation without limitation. With these gifts, God's people are equipped to rule in the created world and worship Him in service.

Paul begins by listing the words of wisdom, knowledge, and faith. Spirit-given wisdom reveals how things should be done among God's people in the world, whereas Spirit-given knowledge shows how people should live with one another and with God. Both of these are related to faith, which is trust in God. Faith is living in the present with appreciation for what God has spoken and done in the past and with anticipation for future words and deeds. Faith joins together wisdom (related to what God has revealed in the world) and knowledge (related to what God has revealed in His word). And as we have already noted, Adam showed wisdom, possessed knowledge, and lived in faith by naming the animals and refusing to eat from the tree at the beginning.

Paul continues by identifying the gifts of healing and miracles. While it is clear that he means healing of the body, the plural noun indicates that he views healing in the holistic sense of joining together. He means healing of restlessness or confusion in one's mind, for example, or distressed relationships, or squandered opportunities. By the Spirit, God works among His people to make them whole and to bind up all parts of their lives, relationships, and world. Likewise, Adam was given the task of completing God's plans for the created world. He was empowered to draw together the substance of that world for new things and discover new possibilities for growth as he submitted to God's word in the garden.[87] Whenever men and women draw on the creation to make new things—art, music, literature, technology—sub-creation or healing in the sense of drawing together occurs.[88]

Related to this is the working of miracles, which recalls the privilege given to Adam to exercise authority over the created world. Miracles are acts that grow the garden or advance God's kingdom. They are not phenomena that elicit *oohs* and *aahs* from people because they are rare, unusual, or spectacular. Miracles are not magic. Nor are they individual blessings done solely for the benefit of those who experience them (though God certainly is not indifferent to how such actions impact the lives of people). The Spirit empowers God's people to participate in the extension of His kingdom as He intended in the beginning when He gave Adam responsibility to increase the garden.[89]

Paul concludes by referring to prophecy, discernment, and spiritual language. The Spirit not only gives the ability to bring things together for new possibilities but also to name what God is doing among His people in the world. As we have noted many times, Adam possessed this ability. According to the Gospel of John, interestingly, naming is also a ministry Jesus performed when he identified Simon as "Peter," Nathanael as a "true Israelite," and Nicodemus as a "teacher of Israel" (John 1–3). Jesus knew (knows) human behavior and the human mind, and as a result of his observation of these men, gave them new names. Prophecy is a gift by which God enables His people to know His mind on specific matters and allows us to participate in naming what He is now doing and will continue to do.

Such naming issues out of discernment and involves the ability to distinguish one thing from another. To distinguish between spirits is to be able to recognize the difference between good from evil. This is especially difficult at times given that good does not necessarily describe what is perfect but what is free.[90] In any case, as we discussed above, only God knows all things, including good and evil, and only His Spirit can distinguish these for us. Related to naming is giving praise. God, by His Spirit, makes it possible for His people to speak with Him without limitation. Thus, not only can we speak His word to one another in prophecy but we can also speak to Him free of language constraints in praise. This type of speech certainly reflects that enjoyed by Adam in the garden when God drew close to him and directly spoke His words to him there.

What Paul says about the fruit and gifts of the Spirit shows that he sees the church not only inhabiting a new garden but actually exhibiting the garden where we live so that the presence of God is experienced and the Spirit provides all that we need to worship Him and reflect His image in the world.

Contentment and the Garden of God

As we have already noted, men and women were created to worship God in freedom. Paul urges the Galatians to use their freedom to love one another (Gal. 5:1–14). Yet as Paul also observes, many remain bound by their own ambitions, appetites, and longings. They remain in jails or prisons of their own making. Is there any physical place that more symbolizes limitation than jail or prison? Such places restrict movement, constrain relationships, and inhibit imagination. A jail is the antithesis of the garden, which represents provision (beauty, strength, relationship, life), purpose (identity, freedom, creativity), and God's presence. Paul knows much about freedom and imprisonment. He says that on several occasions he was arrested and jailed, and the book of Acts concludes with Paul under house arrest in Rome, awaiting a hearing before the emperor.[91]

Paul is convinced that he cannot escape God's loving presence. He writes to the Romans that there is no reality, power, or condition that can remove him from God's love: "I am sure that neither death nor life, nor angels nor rulers, nor things present nor things to come, nor powers, nor height nor depth, nor anything else in all creation, will be able to separate us from the love of God in Christ Jesus our Lord" (Rom. 8:38–39). This means that neither house arrest, nor jail, nor even prison can separate him from the heart of God. Here Paul is not expressing sure confidence in the future grace of God's presence but he is recognizing its present reality.

Paul expresses this same truth to the Ephesians while in prison when he writes that his desire for them is that they may be strengthened by the Spirit to know the love of God and "what is the breadth and length and height and depth" of such love (Eph. 3:16–19). As in Romans, Paul speaks of the infinite nature of God's love at a time when he is bound with chains. In fact, though bound, he sees himself as an ambassador of the gospel who is free to proclaim God's good news despite his circumstances.[92]

Writing to the Philippians from jail, Paul says, "I have learned in whatever situation I am to be content. I know how to be brought low, and I know how to abound. In any and every circumstance, I have learned the secret of facing plenty and hunger, abundance and need" (Phil. 4:11). This is a remarkable statement. How is it possible for him to make this claim? The answer is found in Paul's following words where he says, "I can do all things through Him who strengthens me" (Phil. 4:13). Paul has found contentment through God's strength. Contentment should not be confused with complacency. Complacency connotes carelessness, purposelessness, and even a sense of self-indulgence. It suggests satisfaction with one's situation and an absence of desire or motivation to change that situation, even though it is void of purpose. In other words, complacency describes satisfaction with the status quo. The person who finds himself in such a circumstance is not willing to change it. It may not be good—it may not reach the measure of God's purpose for them—but it is good enough. Rather than satisfaction with the status quo, contentment accepts the circumstances in which one finds oneself because he finds purpose within those circumstances. Contentment is related to purpose.

In this passage, Paul says that he is content because he has found purpose in his circumstances. Though the circumstances in which he finds himself are oppressive—he is in prison—they are not devoid of meaning. As we observed earlier, Viktor Frankl asserts that a sense of purpose was the most essential factor, other than what he describes as mere chance, in surviving the Nazi death camps. By saying that he is content in all circumstances, including those in which he has more than he needs (abundance) and those in which he has less than he desires (want), Paul declares that purpose is not dependent on those circumstances. This is because, for Paul, purpose is relational. It is tied to his relationship with God through the Lord Jesus. Specifically, Paul's purpose may be traced to his encounter with the ascended and glorified Jesus on the Damascus Road and the subsequent divinely given command to preach the gospel to the Gentiles (Acts 9:1–19). Paul is content in prison because he is there on account of his proclamation of the gospel.

Thus, even though some persecute him during his imprisonment through what they say, he knows his purpose: "I am put here for the defense of the gospel." And Christ is proclaimed. This is possible because "I know that through your prayers and the help of the Spirit of Jesus Christ this will turn out for my deliverance" (Phil. 1:16-19). From Paul's words it seems that he has discovered the garden in prison as he experiences God's purpose and provision in the proclamation of the gospel through the presence of the Spirit.

Philippians is not the only letter in which Paul writes about his ministry in terms that recall the garden of God. In Second Corinthians, he concludes a long description of the opposition, hardship, and suffering he has experienced on account of the gospel by writing, "For the sake of Christ, then, I am content with weaknesses, insults, hardships, persecutions, and calamities. For when I am weak, then I am strong" (2 Cor. 12:10). This is a stunning statement. Many of us who read this verse can only shake our heads and ask, "How can you make such a claim, Paul? How can you say you are content with rejection and abuse?" No doubt he would respond that contentment is not complacency. Paul didn't revel in lashings, beatings, and stoning; he didn't welcome danger, hardship, hunger, and thirst. But he is content because he is made strong in them by the presence and power of God's Spirit, who helps him understand that there is a purpose in it "for [the Corinthian's] edification" (2 Cor. 12:19). He sees the fruit of the Spirit in his life and the manifestation of gifts for the benefit of others and he is content that he is in the garden of God.

One wonders when reading Paul's letters. A Roman jail seems an unlikely place to find the garden God planted for Adam in the beginning. Ship wreckage at sea doesn't seem to describe Eden. Dangerous places in the wilderness where robbers pursue, food is scarce, and the weather is cold have nothing in common with the place God first placed Adam. Do they? Not if our picture of the garden is one of pleasure pursuits and idylls, of gratification and self-actualization. If we view Eden as a tropical island caressed by warm breezes or as an uplifting weekend seminar hosted by a well-coifed, reasonable-sounding, higher-consciousness guru, then we will never find it along the Roman roads and in the midst of legionary colonies where Paul preached the gospel. In that case, we will never find it in small jails, cramped cells, or hard floors.

"The Cesspool Was My Garden"

One spring day in 1912, C. Austin Miles was meditating on Mary Magdalene's cold early morning visit to Jesus' tomb as he read John's Gospel account, when he had a vision of the scene.[93] His notes reveal how much he was moved by what he saw: "Out of the mists of the garden comes a form, halting, hesitating, tearful, seeking, turning from side to side ... Faltering, bearing grief in every accent, with tear-dimmed eyes, she whispers, 'If thou hast borne him hence ...' He speaks, and the sound of his voice is so sweet the birds hush their singing. Jesus said to her, "Mary!" Just one word from his lips, and forgotten the heartaches, the long dreary hours ... all the past blotted out in the presence of the Living Present and the Eternal Future." Miles shaped these impressions into the beloved gospel song, "In the Garden":

I come to the Garden alone
While the dew is still on the roses
And the voice I her falling on my ear
The son of God, discloses

Refrain
And He walks with me and He talks with me
And He tells me that I am His own
And the joy we share
as we tarry there
none other has ever known

He speaks and the sound of His voice
Is so sweet that the birds hush their singing
And the melody that He gave to me
Within my heart is ringing

I'd stay in the garden with Him
Though the night around me be falling
But He bids to me
Through the voice of woe
And His voice to me is calling

"In the Garden" is a song about presence and provision found by the most unlikely person, in the most unusual place, at the most unexpected time. It is about Mary Magdalene near a gravesite in the chilled darkness of an early morning. But the song doesn't describe just the garden of the tomb. It describes the garden that waits to be experienced by people today.

In 1952, when George Chen was a young man, he converted to Christianity and soon began to evangelize poor people in rural China.[94] Having a college education and a father who was an industrialist, he was viewed with suspicion by the Communist government—a suspicion that only increased upon his conversion. As a result of his evangelism in the fifties, he was arrested three times by the government and finally sent to a reeducation camp in 1960. He was twenty-six years old and lived the next eighteen years under guard.

Chen's job in the camp was to empty its large outdoor latrine. He was given buckets to scoop out the fetid waste and carry it to nearby fields for fertilizer. And all the while he emptied the cesspool and carried the muck, he quoted scriptures, like Romans 8:28 and 1 Corinthians 13, and sang Austin Miles' song over and over again. The scriptures and song not only comforted him but transported him out of the camp in his spirit. "I felt that I was in the garden with the Lord," he says. "It was there that I learned the true meaning of God's presence." It was a presence that enabled Chen to find blessing in the work that others designed to dehumanize him. And even though he was alone—the "maddening" stench of the cesspool and fear of disease kept everyone, including camp guards, far away from him—God was with him. "I come to the garden alone," he sang. Shunned and isolated, Chen found freedom to pray and praise. "God's presence was with me. I was really in the garden—even in the cesspool."

"Suffering is opposite of good; a cesspool is the opposite of a garden," he says, "but God accomplishes His purpose in both."[95] The garden is wherever God achieves His purpose and provides whatever is needed for it to be done. This doesn't mean the garden is a pleasant or comfortable place to live. Far from it. Sometimes it is harsh and hard and requires every ounce of devotion from us. This was certainly true for Chen, who suffered numerous infections during his years working in the latrine and even had a finger amputated because of disease. His assurance in God's providence did not buckle, however, because he knew where he was. Many prisoners collapsed under the hard labor and others broke down after relentless brainwashing, but Chen endured because, he says, God's presence was with him in prayer, Scripture, and song. God's provision of grace gave him strength, and God's purpose—he looked forward to returning one day to the rural villages of his country and continuing his ministry among the poor—gave him hope.

George Chen exemplifies Paul's declaration, "For the sake of Christ, then, I am content with weaknesses, insults, hardships, persecutions, and calamities. For when I am weak, then I am strong" (2 Cor. 12:10). He says, "I learned that God supports His children in all things and that His grace is sufficient for all that He asks us to do." God gives grace. Paul makes this assertion in view of the word that the Lord has spoken to him: "My grace is sufficient for you, for my power is made perfect in weakness" (2 Cor. 12:9). What Chen was asked to do exceeded his own will or power. The purpose he was given required a power and provision greater than what he possessed. It is a power present in Paul's revelation that "all things work together for good for those who are called according to his purpose." It is a power expressed in the lyrics, "He tells me that I am His own." It is a power that sustained the purpose of God despite the persecution of unnumbered Chinese believers. Chen says that Chinese Christianity grew in response to the persecution. Whereas there were 1 million Christians in 1949 at the beginning of the Cultural Revolution, there were 30 million in 1979 at the end. He says this miracle proves that God works all things together for good in gardens wherever men and women draw on the power of His provision and are willing to let His purposes be accomplished through them.

When George Chen first hiked into the rural mountainous villages as a young man, he thought he was going to a garden-like land. He says that he envisioned open spaces, fresh air, and beauty, and painted a pastel-colored picture in his mind. Instead, he found poverty and hardship. The country was not like the pictures he had seen or like those he had imagined. From a long distance, it looked like a garden, but up close it was hard, desperate, and backward. One might think that after all those years, his desire to work in such a place would have diminished. Yet when Chen was released in 1978, he returned to the same villages where he first started to complete the purpose God originally gave him. And it is there that he continues to experience the presence of God today. We learn from the apostle Paul, Pastor Chen, and many other saints through the years that the garden of God is found wherever God is present and His purpose is being done.

10

The Garden and the City

The last chapters of Revelation provide a final description of the garden of God in relation to the new city of Jerusalem and serve to connect this last book of the Bible with the first. Though the city has garden-like qualities, it is not a garden. This shows that God's future plans will resemble what He has done in the past yet be new and unique. Nonetheless, the resemblances are striking. As we have seen, biblical writers from Moses to the prophets envision a future that resembles the past. Their depictions of the future draw upon the very earliest pictures of Genesis. Not only do they make use of garden imagery to speak of God's yet-to-come desire for His people, but they accent the presence of God, purpose of God, and provision that God makes for His people to fulfill His purpose. They do this to engender anticipation among their readers for a real future by recalling the original past. God's intention is not to have Adam return to the first garden but to lead him forward to a new city that resembles a garden in that it is a place of purpose, provision, and the presence of God.

John describes his vision of the New Jerusalem with words that evoke the brilliance of God's presence. The city shows "the glory of God, its radiance like a most rare jewel, like jasper, clear as crystal" (Rev. 21:11). Most important is the fact that there is no temple in the new city; neither is there sun or moon to give light. The reason is that God himself provides the light of the city through His immediate presence. "And the city has no need of sun or moon to shine on it, for the glory of God gives it light, and its lamp is the Lamb. By its light will the nations walk, and the kings of the earth will bring their glory into it, and its gates will never be shut by day—and there will be no night there" (Rev. 21:24–25). This truth is repeated: "And night will be no more. They will need no light of lamp or sun, for the Lord God will be their light." The nations walk in the presence of God even as God intended Adam to walk with Him in the garden in the beginning and they look upon His face (Rev. 22:4–5). Here John states that the *Lord God* is the light of all the people, just as in the Genesis story it is the *Lord God* who breathed life into Adam, planted the garden, and placed him in it to work and keep it.. God is present in the New Jerusalem in a way that recalls His presence in the Garden of Eden.

So the city is like the first garden in that it is described as "a dwelling place of God with man" (Rev. 21:3). Related to this is the fact that the city is a place where man worships God. John reports that the throne of God is in the midst of the city and "his servants will worship him." And just as the priests of Israel bore the name of God on their headwear, John says the name of God will be written on their foreheads (Rev. 22:3–4). This includes the nations who have been healed by the leaves of the trees of life, meaning they have been reconciled to God and His purpose (Rev. 22:2). The purpose for Adam to work and keep the garden, which we have seen means to worship God, is fulfilled as the nations worship Him in the new city. God's original intention is finally and completely reprised in the New Jerusalem.

Not only this, but the city is built with precious stones. Just as the land surrounding the garden is full of gold, bdellium, and onyx, so also the foundation of the city is made of pure gold and the gates of precious stones. From the midst of the city flows a river that is filled with "the water of life," which waters the Tree of Life that grows on both sides of it. This tree bears "twelve kinds of fruit" and produces leaves "for the healing of the nations." All of this shows that the New Jerusalem is a place of immeasurable wealth and flourishing health for the nations. John says that there will no longer be night. Privation and anguish are banished. There will no longer be ugliness, hunger, or ignorance. Everything that is needed for people to worship God in unity with strength and understanding will be provided for them.

The absence of night speaks of light that washes over all the creation and allows for a profusion of life, which the creation has been anticipating in deliverance from decay (Rom. 8:18–23). It represents that day promised by Isaiah to the exiles of Babylon and fulfilled at the return of the Lord Jesus: "For you shall go out in joy and be led forth in peace; the mountains and the hills before you shall break forth into singing, and all the trees of the field shall clap their hands. Instead of the thorn shall come up the cypress; instead of the brier shall come up the myrtle; and it shall make a name for the Lord, and everlasting sign that shall not be cut off" (Isa. 55:12–13). John sees a new heaven and new earth—an earth free from decay, thorns, and briers, filled with light and healing waters. He sees an earth full of life, led in praise by the sons and daughters of God. He sees a city of proportion where God is present with His people as they lead creation in praise out of the abundance of His provision. He sees a world where the trees of the fields clap their hands.

11

Conclusion

The trees will exult when Adam makes use of the abundant provision of their fruit. When he is inspired in all that he does by their beauty, when he gathers strength from their fruit for nourishment, and when he lives life in obedience to God's word, he is enabled to give names to the animals and ultimately to know and give name to his Creator. In this way, Adam causes the trees of God's creation to rejoice. When he waits upon God for knowledge and gains enlightenment from the one who knows all things, the trees clap their hands.

When God delivered Israel out of Egypt, He led them to a new garden where they would be blessed, live according to His commandments, and give witness to the nations of His goodness and power. The temptation to be like the nations was too strong, however, and the people were forced out of their land of milk and honey in much the same way Adam was forced out of the garden. Nonetheless, the prophets looked forward to a future garden in which all the world would enjoy provision and live with purpose in the presence of God. Isaiah believed that this would happen with the arrival of the Messiah. He envisioned a day when Israel would live an inspired and obedient life in renewed relationship with God, with justice for all. He saw a future day when God's people would know the greater ways and thoughts of God. And, in fact, the Gospels depict Jesus as revealing these ways and thoughts by living such a Spirit-inspired and obedient life before the people for all to see. We do not hear of trees clapping their hands, but we do read of the sea waters settling and the winds easing.

Throughout Jesus' ministry, we see that he was planting the garden everywhere that he went: in the wilderness, by resisting the temptations of the devil and believing God's word to him; among the people, through his teaching on the kingdom of God and with miracles as sterling proof of its presence; at Gethsemane and Golgotha, by committing to God's will and offering forgiveness to the people; and in the midst of his disciples after the resurrection, by breathing upon them with the Holy Spirit.

From Paul's point of view, the people of God themselves become like the trees of the garden when they allow God's Spirit to cultivate fruit in their lives for the benefit of one another. Like the trees that will clap their hands, we give praise to God as we nourish and strengthen each other with the fruit that God gives. In Paul's mind, the Spirit does not only grow fruit in us but God gives garden gifts. Not only are we like trees with fruit, but we are gifts God gives to others. When we gladly receive the gifts that God gives, whether they are Spirit-directed words from people or the people themselves—apostles, prophets, evangelists, pastors-teachers—we are equipped to build the body, advance the kingdom, expand the garden. We can find contentment and experience the garden in the here and now.

The book of Revelation concludes by drawing our attention to the New Jerusalem, in the middle of which is a garden. It sets before us a vision of God's presence as brilliant light that illuminates the whole city. There we see Adam's purpose completed in praise as all the nations worship together. And it is there that all of God's people are sustained by the provision of twelve kinds of fruit from the tree of life on either side of the river. As Adam eats from this fruit, certainly, the trees will clap their hands.

Endnotes

1: INTRODUCTION

1. The population worldwide became more urban than rural in May, 2007. Accessed sciencedaily.com/releases /2007/05/070525000642 on September 1, 2011.

2. Wade Graham, *American Eden: From Monticello to Central Park to Our Backyards: What Our Gardens Tells Us about Who We Are* (New York: HarperCollins, 2011), 93–95.

3. Graham, xiv.

2: THE FIRST GARDEN

4. Nahum M. Sarna, *Genesis: The JPS Torah Commentary* (Philadelphia: The Jewish Publication Society, 1989), 18.

5. An example of this and a favorite of mine is Margaret Greaves' children's book *The Naming*, beautifully illustrated by Pauline Baynes (the original illustrator of C.S. Lewis' *Chronicles of Narnia* books).

6. *Paradise Lost*, Book IV, Lines 327–334.

7. Kirsten Nielsen says that the garden trees "clearly reflect the Canaanite holy grove with the holy trees at the life-giving spring, the place where man participates in the divine life" (*There Is Hope for a Tree: The Tree as Metaphor in Isaiah* [Sheffield: Sheffield Academic Press, 1989], 81).

8. These needs generally correspond to "the four basic senses of the human spirit as it responds to God" in worship, identified by Allen Ross. These senses include the intellectual, aesthetic, corporate, and moral. See *Recalling the Hope of Glory: Biblical Worship from the Garden to the New Creation* (Grand Rapids: Kregel Publications, 2006), 57–60. N.T. Wright sees human need as fourfold as well, involving the desire for justice, spirituality, relationship, and beauty, in *Simply Christian: Why Christianity Makes Sense* (New York: HarperOne, 2006).

9. Thus, the word *'ābad* describes the work of Levites and priests in the sanctuary (Num. 3:7–8; 4:23; 7:5; 8:11; 16:9; 18:5–6, 21, 23), while *šāmar* describes fidelity to the commandments and stipulations of the covenant by the people and their leaders in relation to such things as the Sabbath (Exod. 12:17; 23:15; 34:12; Lev. 19:3, 30; Deut. 5:12; Isa. 56:4) and Passover (Exod. 23:15; 34:18; Deut. 16:1). They are found together in Num. 3:7–8; 8:26; and 18:5–6 to describe the duties of the Levites.

10. John H. Sailhamer, *The Pentateuch as Narrative: A Biblical-Theological Commentary*, Library of Biblical Interpretation (Grand Rapids: Zondervan, 1992), 100–101.

11. Peter J. Leithart, *Defending Constantine: The Twilight of an Empire and the Dawn of Christendom* (Downers Grove: IVP Academic, 2010), 333.

12. Viktor E. Frankl, *Man's Search for Meaning* (Boston: Beacon Press, 2006), 76.

13. It is epistemological and is foundational to his relationship with God.

14. C.S. Lewis, *A Preface to Paradise Lost* (London: Oxford University Press, 1942), 65.

15. Vicki Hearne, *Adam's Task: Calling Animals by Name* (Pleasantville, NY: The Akadine Press, 2000), 170–71.

16. Gen. 1:3–10.

17. Gen. 1:11–22.

18. Wade Graham, *American Eden: From Monticello to Central Park to Our Backyards: What Our Gardens Tell Us about Who We Are* (New York: HarperCollins, 2011), xiii–xiv.

19. J.R.R. Tolkien described his own literary creation of Middle-earth with all of its history and mythology as a work of sub-creation. See Bradley Birzer, *Tolkien's Sanctifying Myth*.

20. Although I describe this as a covenant, I recognize that it does not contain the specific elements of ancient covenants or treaties. The Hittite covenant model that informs biblical covenants such as the Mosaic covenant is not evident here. Still, the fact that God makes a declaration to himself to accomplish a particular goal—to make Adam in His image—establishes the foundation for all of His actions afterward and suggests a covenant to which He commits himself. See Delbert R. Hillers, *Covenant: The History of a Biblical Idea* (Baltimore/London: The Johns Hopkins University Press, 1969), for a complete treatment of covenant in the Old Testament.

21. Graham, xii.

22. See Robert Banks' *God the Worker: Journeys into the Mind, Heart, and Imagination of God* (Claremont: Albatross Books, 1992) where the author places the biblical

metaphor of the gardener alongside other well-known pictures of God.

23. Frankl, 37–38.

24. Gen. 1: 3, 10, 13, 18, 21, 25, 31.

25. I believe that God's original intention was for Adam to know Him through His personal presence and good creation. Prior to Adam's disobedience of God's command, this way of knowing God would have increasingly led to a deep and intimate relationship with Him. As many have pointed out, natural theology today provides a limited understanding of God that can only be fully grasped through the revelation of God's Son. This is because the creation has been affected adversely by Adam's rebellion and cannot provide an unaltered way to knowledge of God.

26. See Exod. 18:4; Deut. 33:7, 26, 29; Pss. 10:14; 20:2; 33:20; 70:5; 115:9–11; 121:1–2; 124:8; 146:5; Hos. 13:9.

27. Hugh Ross, *The Creator and the Cosmos: How the Latest Scientific Discoveries Reveal God*, 3rd expanded edition (Colorado Springs: NavPress, 2001), 124.

28. Hugh Ross, *Beyond the Cosmos: What Recent Discoveries in Astrophysics Reveal about the Glory and Love of God*, revised and updated (Colorado Springs: NavPress, 1996), 200.

29. Juliette Aristides, *Classical Drawing Atelier: A Contemporary Guide to Traditional Studio Practice* (New York: Watson-Guptill Publications, 2006), 19–20. Aristides defines the ratio: "Mathematically, the golden ratio produces a logically ordered progressive relationship between two parts such that the proportion of the larger part to the smaller part is the same as the whole to the larger part … The key is that the golden ratio is the only type of ratio whereby the whole and the part relate to each

other in the same way. This is harmony." (20) Stated in sequential terms, it is known as the Fibonacci sequence: 1+1=2, 1+2=3, 2+3=5, 3+5=8, 5+8=13 … This is exactly the growth pattern found in nature.

30. It should be noted that goodness does not denote perfection. In fact, Terence Fretheim reminds us that God's good creation was "characterized by 'wildness,' randomness, risks such as water and the law of gravity, and the potential for ever-new developments in the natural order … Much potential for pain and suffering existed in the prehuman, pre-sin world" (*Creation Untamed: The Bible, God, and Natural Disasters* [Grand Rapids: Baker Academic, 2010], 3).

31. Lewis, 66–69.

32. Lewis, 73.

33. Lewis, 75–76. He says that the story of creation and Adam is a story about hierarchy.

34. "Adam's fall was a renunciation of war, a capitulation to the enemy, a failure to defend his bride and to take up the war of Yahweh … Adam was formed as a king-in-training, and combat with the serpent was his first test. Had he passed the test, he would presumably have been given the fruit of the tree of knowledge and ascended to share in the rule of his heavenly Father, the human king beside the High King" (Leithart, 334). An aspect of Adam's privation, in other words, is that he loses the position that God intended him to have. Instead of being a general/king, he becomes a private.

35. Lewis, 64.

36. Rom. 8:20–23.

3: ABRAHAM'S GARDEN JOURNEY

37. In the earlier story of Noah, we read that God renews His provision for His people, commands them to increase, and establishes a new covenant of relationship with all living creatures after the waters recede. Yet we are not told that Noah and his family lived a life of purpose and manifested God's image in the earth. In fact, as soon as the covenant is recorded, we read that Noah lay drunk in his tent and was dishonored by his youngest son. In other words, the place where Noah lived after the flood is not described in a way that recalls the first garden.

38. Gen. 22:1.

4: THE EXODUS AND THE GARDEN

39. Norman C. Habel describes several biblical views of the land in his book, *The Land Is Mine: Six Biblical Land Ideologies* (Minneapolis: Fortress, 1995).

40. Exod. 3:8, 17; Num. 13:25–28, 14:5–10; Deut. 8:6–10, 11:8–12.

41. *TDOT*, vol. 3, 128. See also Nathan MacDonald, *What Did the Ancient Israelites Eat? Diet in Biblical Times* (Grand Rapids/Cambridge: Eerdmans, 2008). Whereas honey was a treat in the diet of ancient Israelites, milk was a staple food source. It was mostly drawn from goats and made into cheese. It was not often used for drinking since goats only produce milk for half the year and it easily spoils in warm weather. Often cheese is described in the Bible as a food offered to guests and seen as a tangible expression of hospitality (35–40).

42. Exod. 5:1; 8:1; 8:20; 9:1; 10:3.

43. Samuel Terrien, *The Elusive Presence: Toward a New Biblical Theology*, Religious Perspectives, vol. 26 (San Francisco: Harper & Row Publishers, 1978), 124.

44. Deut. 30:11–20.

45. Lev. 27:34; 11:1–47; 17:10–16.

46. It is noteworthy that this is exactly how Israel interpreted the Assyrian exile of the eighth century and the Babylonian exile a century or so later.

47. Prefatory Notes, Tolkien Official Calendar 2011, Illustrated by Cor Blok (New York: HarperCollins, 2010), n.p.

48. Exodus 25–30 may be divided into seven speeches (25:1–30:10; 30:11–16; 30:17–21; 30:22–33; 30:34–38; 31:1–11; and 31:12–17) with the first six focused on the building of the tabernacle and the seventh on the Sabbath. Allen Ross comments, "There were six days to make the earth and six steps in the instructions to make the tabernacle; and then there was rest ... So there is a deliberate attempt to show that the construction of the sanctuary paralleled the work of creation, as if to say, this was God's new creation of his dwelling place on earth" (*Recalling the Hope of Glory: Biblical Worship from the Garden to the New Creation* [Grand Rapids: Kregel Publications, 2006], 87–88). On the construction of the tabernacle, see Exodus 25–31; 37:17–24; and Numbers 8:1–4.

49. Exod. 25:10–40; 27:1–8; 40:24.

50. The almond tree was the earliest tree to blossom in the spring and give evidence of new life.

51. Deut. 10:1–5; Exod. 7:8–12; Num. 17:1–11.

52. Ross, *Recalling the Hope of Glory*, 250.

5: THE TREES WILL CLAP THEIR HANDS

53. Though the Hebrew words for *thorns* and *thistles* in Genesis 3 are not the same ones used by the prophet in Isaiah 55, the imagery is the same.

54. Much has been written about the servant of Isaiah, and different views concerning his identity have been proposed. Whether or not the servant is the prophet himself, the people as a whole, or an anticipated Messiah, he brings about the fulfillment of God's desire for the nations to know Him (purpose) through the help of the Spirit (provision). Isaiah 42 emphasizes justice for the nations by using the word *justice* (*mišpat*) three times in the first four verses of the passage.

55. The creation miracles of Jesus described in the Gospels show the reestablishment of Adam's authority over nature as well as the release of nature to give praise to God by enabling Jesus' ministry to proceed unhindered. See discussion on this subject below.

56. 1 Cor. 15:42–49; Rom. 5:12–6:14.

57. Chapters 25–32.

58. Chapters 26–28.

59. Ezekiel's fluid use of different images, passages of Scripture, traditions, and broad knowledge of events makes it hard to determine his intention with certainty. Moshe Greenberg describes the prophet as a polymath given his massive knowledge of literature, traditions, and contemporary events. He notes the ambiguous nature of this passage when he writes, "Doubtless the most difficult aspect of this oracle is its polymorphism: persons and settings keep changing from stanza to stanza. [The first stanza's] creature perfect in form, wisdom, and beauty—but not called divine—is transformed in [the second stanza] into a cherub. The creature is set in the Garden of Eden, the cherub on the

118

holy mountain of God" (*Ezekiel 21–37: A New Translation with Introduction and Commentary*, The Anchor Bible [New York: Doubleday, 1997], 589). For Ezekiel's vast knowledge, see 395–396.

60. Greenberg translates the phrase as "sealer of proportion," meaning that he was perfectly proportioned (580).

61. Translation from Greenberg, 579.

62. Exod. 28:17–20.

6: A LAND OF WINE

63. Num. 13.

64. "The frequent references to wine in the Old Testament suggest that it was not only the principal alcoholic beverage, but the principal drink" (Nathan MacDonald, *What Did the Ancient Israelites Eat? Diet in Biblical Times* [Grand Rapids/Cambridge: Eerdmans, 2008], 22).

65. John R. Levison writes, "This is a breathtaking vision that begins at the beginning of time and concludes in the certain future, when life comes full circle, when Israel receives the spirit within, when bone connects to bone, when the homeland is tilled and Eden restored" (*Filled with the Spirit* [Grand Rapids/Cambridge: Eerdmans, 2009], 102).

66. Joel 2:18–27.

7: JOB'S HEDGE

67. Job 1:1; 2:3; 6:24; 7:20–21; 8:20; 9:17–22; 12:4; 13:23; 19:6; 27:6; 29:1f, 31.

68. Job 42:7–8.

69. Eliphaz: 4:7–11; 15:12–16; 22:21–30; Bildad: 8:3–7; Zophar: 11:13–15.

70. Job 6:24f; 9:15, 20; 13:18, 23; 23:7–12; 27:2–6.

71. Matt. 4:3–7; Luke 4:3–4.

72. Job 42:2–3.

73. Eliphaz, chp.5; Bildad, chp.8; Zophar, chp.11.

74. The description of the Tree of the Knowledge of Good and Evil in Genesis is an example of merism, a word or phrase that signifies a set or totality of things. Thus, good and evil refers to "everything." What is knowledge of good and evil? It is the ability to make independent judgment on human welfare without divine direction.

8: JESUS AND THE GARDEN

75. Matt. 11:12. Many translations read, "The kingdom has suffered violence but the violent take it by force." Both translations are possible, due to the passive/middle voice of the verb. Given the previous passage in which Jesus prepares the disciples for opposition and persecution, the middle-voice reading given here is best.

76. For an historical treatment of these miracles, see Graham Twelftree's *Jesus the Miracle Worker: A Historical and Theological Study* (Downers Grove: IVP, 1999), 314–330.

77. Mark 4:35–41; 6:45–52.

78. Geraint Vaughn Jones, *Art and Truth of the Parables* (London: SPCK, 1964), 177.

79. Kenneth E. Bailey, *Jacob and the Prodigal: How Jesus Retold Israel's Story* (Downers Grove: IVP, 2003), 102.

80. Matt. 26:39, 42.

81. Howard Hageman, "Paradise Now" in *Bread and Wine: Readings for Lent and Easter* (Farmington: The Plough Publishing House, 2003), 277.

82. Hageman, 278.

9: PAUL'S EXPERIENCE OF THE GARDEN

83. John 13:34–35. New Testament scholars believe the teaching recorded in chapters 13–17 represents that given by Jesus over a period of days or longer. See, for example, Ben Witherington, III, *Making a Meal of It: Rethinking the Theology of the Lord's Supper* (Waco: Baylor University Press, 2007), 64.

84. This recalls Frankl's observation noted above that meaning always is unique to each individual and is expressed in particular ways. See *Man's Search for Meaning* (Boston: Beacon Publications, 2006), 109.

85. In his sermon to Cornelius, Peter summarizes the entirety of Jesus' ministry by saying that he "went about doing good." Jesus did what God his Father desired in the way that he desired (Acts 10:38).

86. Allen Ross, *Recalling the Hope of Glory: Biblical Worship from the Garden to the New Creation* (Grand Rapids: Kregel Publications), 90.

87. Terence Fretheim observes that creation requires development and God enables both creation itself and His creatures to participate in continuing creation. See

Creation Untamed: The Bible, God, and Natural Disasters (Grand Rapids: Baker Academic, 2010), 19–37.

88. Bradley Birzer writes that Tolkien believed creativity was the expression of the divine image in mankind. "God, as Creator, poured forth the gift of creativity to men, the creatures created in his own image. Only God can create in the primary sense, i.e., by bringing something into being out of nothing. Man, however, can sub-create by molding the material of creation into works of beauty" (*J.R.R. Tolkien's Sanctifying Myth: Understanding Middle-earth* [Wilmington: ISI Books, 2002], x). Later Birzer observes, "Man is nothing, Tolkien believed, if not a subcreator made in the image of the true creator. God places each uniquely created individual in a certain time, in a certain place, with certain gifts, for a certain reason" (110).

89. Fretheim, 19–37.

90. Fretheim, 12–17.

91. Phil. 1:12–14; 2 Cor. 11:23; Eph. 3:1; Acts 28:16, 30.

92. Eph. 6:20. Richard Cassidy writes, "Paul was the ambassador of his Lord, chosen for a mission that presumed his reliability and entrusted with a profound message. However, instead of being received with high protocol, he was received into chained imprisonment. Nevertheless, he remained steadfastly committed to proclaiming the gospel entrusted to him" (*Christians and Roman Rule in the New Testament* [New York: The Crossroad Publishing Company, 2001], 99).

93. For details on the story behind Miles' "In the Garden," see Robert J. Morgan, *Then Sings My Soul: 150 of the World's Greatest Hymn Stories* (Nashville: Thomas Nelson, 2003).

94. The information for the following description comes from a personal interview with Pastor Chen in Hong Kong, October 2, 2008. A narrative account may be read in *Still Red* by Georgina Sam and David Wang (Hong Kong: Asian Outreach International, 2008).

95. Victor Frankl observes that it is important for people to be able to find meaning in suffering. "Man's main concern is not to gain pleasure or to avoid pain but rather to see a meaning in his life. That is why man is even ready to suffer, on the condition, to be sure, that his suffering has meaning" (113).

Bibliography

Aristides, Juliette, *Classical Drawing Atelier: A Contemporary Guide to Traditional Studio Practice* (New York: Watson-Guptill Publications, 2006).

Bailey, Kenneth E., *Jacob and the Prodigal: How Jesus Retold Israel's Story* (Downers Grove: IVP, 2003).

Banks, Robert, *God the Worker: Journeys into the Mind, Heart, and Imagination of God* (Claremont: Albatross Books, 1992).

Birzer, Bradley J., *J.R.R. Tolkien's Sanctifying Myth: Understanding Middle-earth* (Wilmington: ISI Books, 2002).

Cassidy, Richard, *Christians and Roman Rule in the New Testament* (New York: The Crossroad Publishing Company, 2001).

Charlesworth, James, ed., *The Old Testament Pseudepigrapha*, vols. 1–2 (New York: Doubleday, 1983–85).

Chen, George, *Private interview*, Hong Kong, October 2, 2008.

Frankl, Viktor E., *Man's Search for Meaning* (Boston: Beacon Press, 1959).

Fretheim, Terence E., *Creation Untamed: The Bible, God, and Natural Disasters* (Grand Rapids: Baker Academic, 2010).

Goldingay, John, *Old Testament Theology: Israel's Gospel, vol. 1 (Downers Grove: IVP Academic, 2003).*

Graham, Wade, *American Eden: From Monticello to Central Park to Our Backyards: What Our Gardens Tell Us about Who We Are (New York: HarperCollins, 2011).*

Greenberg, Moshe, *Ezekiel 21–37: A New Translation with Introduction and Commentary, The Anchor Bible (New York: Doubleday, 1997).*

Habel, Norman C., *The Land Is Mine: Six Biblical Land Ideologies (Minneapolis:Fortress Press, 1995).*

Hageman, Howard, *"Paradise Now" in Bread and Wine (Farmington: The Plough Publishing House, 2003).*

Hearne, Vicki, *Adam's Task: Calling Animals by Name (Pleasantville, NY: The Akadine Press, 2000).*

Hillers, Delbert R., *Covenant: The History of a Biblical Idea (Baltimore/ London: The Johns Hopkins University Press, 1969).*

Jones, Geraint Vaughn, *Art and Truth of the Parables (London: SPCK, 1964).*

Leithart, Peter J., *Defending Constantine: The Twilight of an Empire and the Dawn of Christendom (Downers Grove: IVP Academic, 2010).*

Levison, John R., *Filled with the Spirit (Grand Rapids/Cambridge: Eerdmans, 2009).*

Lewis, C.S., *A Preface to Paradise Lost (Oxford: Oxford University Press, 1942).*

MacDonald, Nathan, *What Did the Ancient Israelites Eat? Diet in Biblical Times (Grand Rapids: Eerdmans, 2008).*

Miles, C. Austin, *"In the Garden"\ (1912).*

Milton, John, *Paradise Lost, into. Edward Le Comte (New York: New American Library, 1961).*

Morgan, Robert J., *Then Sings My Soul: 150 of the World's Greatest Hymn Stories* (Nashville: Thomas Nelson, 2003).

Nielsen, Kirsten, *There Is Hope for a Tree: The Tree as Metaphor in Isaiah* (Sheffield: Sheffield Academic Press, 1989).

Ross, Allen P., *Recalling the Hope of Glory: Biblical Worship from the Garden to the New Creation* (Grand Rapids: Kregel Publications, 2006).

Ross, Hugh, *The Creator and the Cosmos: How the Latest Scientific Discoveries Reveal God*, 3rd expanded edition (Colorado Springs: NavPress, 2001).

_____, *Beyond the Cosmos: What Recent Discoveries in Astrophysics Reveal about the Glory and Love of God*, revised and updated (Colorado Springs: NavPress, 1996).

Sailhamer, John H., *The Pentateuch as Narrative: A Biblical-Theological Commentary* (Grand Rapids: Zondervan Publishing House, 1992).

Sam, Georgina, and David Wang, *Still Red* (Hong Kong: Asian Outreach International, 2008).

Sarna, Nahum M., *Genesis: The JPS Torah Commentary* (Philadelphia: Jewish Publication Society, 1989).

Terrien, Samuel, *The Elusive Presence: Toward a New Biblical Theology*, Religious Perspectives, vol. 26 (San Francisco: Harper & Row Publishers, 1978).

Theological Dictionary of the Old Testament

Twelftree, Graham H., *Jesus the Miracle Worker: A Historical & Theological Study* (Downers Grove: IVP, 1999).

Witherington, Ben III, *Making a Meal of It: Rethinking the Theology of the Lord's Supper* (Waco: Baylor University Press, 2007).

Wright, N.T., *Simply Christian: Why Christianity Makes Sense* (New York: HarperOne, 2006).

Scripture Index

Made in the USA
San Bernardino, CA
21 November 2017